Conversations With Top Real Estate Investors Vol. 2

With contributing Authors

Bob Snyder

Christal Bowlby

Julie Hudetz Dale

Darren Davis

Nate Lambert

Susa Lindsey

Seth McGovern

Michael Myer

Celest Secrist

Michelle Stiff

Briant & Jamie Stringham

Tim Vreeland

Perran & Loretta Wetzel

Josh White

Hugh & Jessica Zaretsky

Woody Woodward

Warning—Disclaimer

The purpose of this book is to educate and inspire. This book is not intended to give advice or make promises or guarantees that anyone following the ideas, tips, suggestions, techniques or strategies will have the same results as the people listed throughout the stories contained herein. The author, publisher and distributor(s) shall have neither liability nor responsibility to anyone with respect to any loss or damage caused, or alleged to be caused, directly or indirectly by the information contained in this book.

ISBN: 978-0-9982340-1-4

Table of Contents

Introduction

Have you ever wanted to be sitting at the table when major real estate transaction were happening just to be able to glean insider information? If your answer was, "Yes" then this book is dedicated to you. You are going to be like a fly on the wall as top real estate investors are being interviewed and sharing their tips and strategies to being successful. These are honest and raw interviews with the intent to inspire you to follow your real estate dreams.

Bob Snyder

Renatus was founded and is led by 25-year entrepreneur, Mr. Bob Snyder. As CEO and President, Mr. Snyder is responsible for day-to-day company operations, affiliate marketing program expansion, course curriculum evaluation and renewal, practitioner-instructor recruiting, and month-over-month increased sales performance.

Mr. Snyder began his entrepreneurial journey over 25 years ago with the desire to leave a positive mark on the world. Establishing himself as a marketing leader, he gained first-hand knowledge of what drives marketing and team-building success. Mr. Snyder built and managed sales organizations with tens of thousands of individuals, achieved top status in multiple companies, and became a top income earner in the direct selling industry. He has freely shared his formula for success as he served on more than a dozen leadership counsels and advisory boards in the direct sales industry, received recognition in national publications as an expert in his field and has personally mentored over a dozen marketers to become seven-figure earners.

After years of building and growing marketing teams, Mr. Snyder's vision transitioned him into developing companies to expand the entrepreneurial spirit that has made this country the world's economic leader. He has founded and co-founded dozens of companies that have collectively produced hundreds of millions of dollars in revenue. His real estate company completed over 2,500 real estate transactions while his former education company trained over 60,000 entrepreneurs on the subject of real estate investing and business ownership.

Contact Info:
www.MyRenatus.com

Shannon:

According to Forbes magazine, real estate is one of the top three ways that people become wealthy. As a real estate expert, why do you feel that this is the case?

Bob:

Because real estate is one of the three basic human needs: food, water, and shelter. There's always going to be a demand for real estate. Tech companies come and go, financial companies come and go, media companies come and go, but real estate is constant, and we are always going to have a need for it. Those individuals who position themselves with the right kind of properties are always going to be able to generate monthly cash flow.

Shannon:

Is that what inspired you to get into real estate: supply and demand?

Bob:

No. What inspired me to get into real estate was my wife. She dragged me kicking and screaming into real estate.

Here's the thing, I didn't understand it, and we always fear what we don't understand. I had been raised with the idea that a secure retirement required investments in the stock market. The problem was that I kept giving money to my broker and I continued to GET broker!

My wife was increasingly frustrated that we kept losing money on Wall Street, even from our conservative mutual fund investments. They weren't producing any kind of a sustainable return. By contrast, her mother and father invested in real estate while she was growing up. They made a habit of buying properties, paying them off, selling them, and buying others to build their portfolios. They developed cash flows that would take care of them in their retirement. Today, my father-in-law is eighty-eight years old and he and his wife live very comfortably from their paid-for real estate. The proof's in the pudding.

So, after losing a bunch of money on Wall Street my wife came to me and said, "Listen. We need to be in real estate. It's the way to build and secure our future and our kids' future. It's not Wall Street. It's not the stock market and it's not this other nonsense that you've been dealing with." Unfortunately, I was stubborn. I did not want to listen to her, but she was right and the last thing in the world I ever wanted was to tell her that she was right.

Shannon:
Now, looking back, you think, "Thank Goodness she was right."

Bob:
Yes, and think about what happened as a result of that, but it didn't happen overnight. She worked on me and worked on me, and I kept saying no. Then she finally came to me and she said, "Listen, Bob. I found this great little duplex. Its owner occupied on one side with a tenant on the other side, so the owner really fixed it up nice. The property is for sale by owner. We can get it a decent deal. It'll cash flow after we get a mortgage on it. You won't have to deal with it. I will manage it. I just need your support because if I don't do this I'm going to regret this rest of my life and you wouldn't want that, would you?" I mean, come on, what do you say to that?

Shannon:
You say, "You know, honey, I think we should get into real estate."

Bob:
I said, "You're absolutely right, but if this thing goes south I don't know if I'll be able to resist saying I told you so."

About a year later we were taking a look at the property's rents and depreciation schedule. All I could think was, "Holy smokes, we've got somebody living in our investment property who works all month long to make sure that we're the first one that gets paid. What an amazing business model." Then we get all these tax write offs, and the property was appreciating in value. This is phenomenal! It was one of those moments where I was like, "Wow, I'm glad I thought of it."

Shannon:
So when you were sitting in that real estate office, did she turn to you and say, "I told you so," or did she just say, "Bob, I am so glad you thought of this."

Bob:
You know, it's funny, Holly was really good about it. She just said, "You know what? You just needed to see it. You just needed to see it and do it," and she was right. All I could think to say was that we need to be doing a whole heck of a lot more of this, and that's what started our real estate investing career.

Back then we were so green, so naïve, we didn't understand real estate. We didn't understand wholesale buying opportunities. We did what 99.9 percent of the investors in this country do: go out, find a property, pay almost full price for it, put a tenant in the darn thing, and then you pray and hope that it's going to cash flow sometime in the next ten years. That's where our investing career started, but it gave me the bug and I had a desire to learn more, to grow in that business, to learn creative real estate strategies so that I could acquire properties for pennies on the dollar or buy them without any money out of pocket. I understood that with the right knowledge and drive to be a successful investor, I would never have to worry about money again.

Shannon:
Now, you've got all this knowledge and you've got years of experience, if someone wanted to get started in real estate, what would you recommend is the very first thing they do?

Bob:
The very first thing they need to do is get educated. That's just it. It's a business whereby if you know what you're doing you can make a whole lot of money and if you don't you can lose a whole lot of money. There is absolutely no ceiling on your income—the sky's the limits. You can become a millionaire, a billionaire, and I'm sure that down the road there will even be trillionaire real estate investors. The problem is, there's no floor either.

Shannon:

Yeah, I guess, if there's no ceiling...

Bob:

Yeah, if you don't know what you're doing, you can lose money. That's the biggest thing. You've got to get educated so that you have at least a common baseline of information, so you know how to fall in love with the deal and not the property. You need to know how to work the numbers and ensure that you are making a good, prudent business decision that's going to be profitable for you. The next thing is you've got to take action. I see too many individuals who fall into the category of what I call, educated derelicts. They're so versed on all sorts of different real estate strategies and different ideas, but they don't do anything with it. It's just fear that holds them back.

Shannon:

What do you do to get over that fear?

Bob:

Again, get educated. Education builds competency and when you feel competent about something you are more likely to take action. Action helps you to overcome fear, so the real formula for success is for a person to get educated and then to get busy. Education without action will not produce results.

For example, there are three types of students: the drop outs, the graduates, and the eternal. Those who keep learning and never start applying what they have learned continue to make up a larger and larger segment of our population. They are paralyzed by fear.

Let me give you an old acronym for fear

False

Evidence

Appearing

Real.

I believe that wealth is a mindset. Individuals start a conversation in their own mind that leads them to a certain belief, that belief either prevents them from moving forward or actually compels them to move forward. How they see risk plays an important role. Somewhere in their internal dialogue is a conversation about risk. When their focus shifts to all that can go wrong with an opportunity, they talk themselves out of moving forward with that opportunity.

That's why we build local communities of real estate investors all across the country. These local groups get together on a regular basis to talk about their real estate deals and what's going on in their business. When you've got somebody brand new who is fearful about fixing and flipping or building cash flow, it makes all the difference in the world to immerse them in an active community of investors. Surrounded by investors who are making offers, doing deals, and making money, a student gains confidence to make it happen for themselves.

At Renatus, we surround our students with examples of success so that they can get a realistic view of what it takes to succeed. In colleges and universities, students are stuck on the degree treadmill. They risk nothing and just keep going from class to class to class and degree to degree to degree. The lack of real world experience is the challenge with higher education.

Shannon:
Which becomes their new job.

Bob:
Yeah. It's not until they get into the real world that they start to experience anything. Believe me, I am a big proponent of education in whatever form that it can possibly come from. Unfortunately, higher education is letting more people down. They're getting degrees in fields of study that they will never make a living in and sometimes it enables them to just stay in that "safe" environment where they never take action which is why student loan debt continues to increase and student outcomes continue to decrease.

Shannon:
So, how do you change that?

Bob:

Specialized knowledge. It's unfortunate that the world of academia will never accept our type of educators because many of them don't have a college degree. Heck, some of them barely got their GED, but they are all successful, profitable investors. As for me, I got right into the world of business and by the time my friends were all graduating from college, I was making two to three times the money they were making.

Shannon:

How did you get educated? What did you do?

Bob:

You're going to love this story. I started my career in sales and marketing and then because of the frustration I dealt with working for someone else, I stepped into the wonderful world of owning and operating my own businesses. I had learned over the years how to build training platforms. I knew how to build sales teams. I knew how to create and build companies and I had a business partner who was also a seasoned entrepreneur. Together we were involved in a travel company but, after 9/11, nobody wanted to talk about travel; everybody was hunkered down and fearful of getting around the world. Our travel business really tanked. I did about everything I possibly could to get the wings back on the plane and make that thing fly again, but it just wasn't happening.

It was at that point that I had a conversation with my partner. I said, "Listen. Sometimes the best way to protect an opportunity is to create a new one." We owned real estate but we didn't understand wholesale buying or a lot about the real estate industry. I suggested we create an educational company centered on real estate investing. Then we hired the big gurus to come in and teach our people how to invest. The idea was that while our students learned, we would learn. What an idea, right?

That's where it all started. But the challenge was that the gurus we hired to teach students, students who paid good money to be in those classes, often refused to teach! They only wanted to whet the appetite of the listener so that they could up sell them to their own courses.

Shannon:
Oh, wow.

Bob:
So I talked to a friend of mine who had a PhD in Education. I told him we had a problem we needed to get beyond. Somehow we had to create a true learning environment instead of the ridiculous circus sales environment that our competitors used. He said he could help and we hired him.

He worked with us, and our staff, very closely for about a year. We brought in subject matter experts (SMEs) to help us take a good look at the real estate industry and construct our curriculum. We went out and organized focus groups from those who had paid money to gurus, both those who had and had not invested yet. All those focus groups assisted us in understanding what holds people back from investing.

We found there were four principle reasons for not investing: I don't have the time, I don't have the money/credit, I don't have the knowledge, or I'm just afraid. Those were the most common excuses. I view them as the excuses that cause failure.

Shannon:
I think we can say that for every aspect of our lives.

Bob:
Yes, we can. As soon as you start doing something, all of a sudden you say, "Hey, that wasn't so bad." I liken it to people who are W-2 employees. Most are fearful about whatever new thing they take on in life. For example, let's go back to the first day they started a new job or a new career. Were they a little intimidated? Were they a little nervous? If they're honest, they're always going to say yes. Fast forward six months. By then they have a pretty good handle on it. Most would say that they had gotten really good at their job and feel confident in it. The challenge is that they rarely ever feel like they are getting paid what they are worth?

We all go through that process. Fear is overcome through action.

We've got to get people in an environment that helps them to take one step after another. That's another thing I learned from Dr. Paul Ripicke. He taught us about the Instructional System design (ISD) methodology for curriculum building. It's what every major college and university in the country uses to build their curriculum paths and focus on student outcomes.

We thought, "well, if Harvard and Yale and Princeton are using this, we can use it too," so we went out and worked with individuals who were actual full-time investors in a specific strategy and we brought them on board. We worked with them to help us craft these classes, and then we taught them how to teach, and then we fired all the gurus. From that point forward, we had real-life investors standing up in front of our classrooms teaching our students. We forbid any of those instructors to ever sell anything in class because we knew that that would be a massive conflict of interest because the minute they started selling they would stop teaching.

Shannon:
Was there one type of person or personality that seemed to be most drawn to your classes or had the type of personality to be the most successful?

Bob:
It's not the personality, it's the circumstance. That's the one thing that all of our students shared; there was a heightened level of dissatisfaction with where they were. It didn't matter whether they were in a successful profession or they were just out of college struggling to make ends meet. They all had a level of dissatisfaction, whether it was enough time with their family, or a good enough future, or they were just sick and tired of working for a boss that didn't appreciate them. They all had a level of dissatisfaction. Again, wealth is a mindset. We just needed to give them hope.

Even for the staff who work here at Renatus, there's a huge shift in their mental framework. They may come in believing they need to contribute each month to their 401(k), but they end up learning how to do creative real estate investing to build their own wealth that they can control. It's pretty exciting to see that the staff members are also embracing the classes and getting out and doing their own deals.

Shannon:

It's kind of exciting because your employees could turn into full-time real estate investors and then you get to hire new employees and teach them, wouldn't you think?

Bob:

You know, there's always that thought in the back of your mind that, key people are going to start making so much money they're going to leave you. I encourage it, but over and over and over again I've got that same group of people who say, "You know what? This is what I want to do for the rest of my life." Renatus is a cause more than it is a job to them because they see the benefits that are showing up in other people's lives and that gives them a great deal of self-satisfaction.

Shannon:

Do you think students should find one real estate investing strategy and stick with that and become an expert, or do you think they should diversify?

Bob:

One of our favorite classes is understanding your investor ID because everybody's different. For example, some individuals have no problem going out there and buying property that they're going to put lower-income tenants into. They're just happy to get that check from the government every single month. Other individuals believe that if they wouldn't live in it, then they won't own it. We have different types of personalities and mindsets. They can all make money in real estate.

What we've got to do is figure out what their investor ID is: do they want quick turn real estate for lump sum cash returns or do they want to build cash flow over time with a nice, passive income from the property? I always tell people, once you figure out your investor ID, then you learn everything you possibly can about that strategy and you focus on that to become an expert.

But, you never stay stuck with just one strategy because markets shift and change. That's why we teach so many different strategies in Renatus. No matter what is happening with the market, no matter what is happening with the economy, if there's a shift or an adjustment in the real estate business and you haven't secured yourself with an understanding of different ways to get the same thing done, you're going to find yourself on the outside looking in and saying, "Well, gee, the economy's bad, so, the opportunity's gone." Not true, my educated students crushed it through the Great Recession. They made money hand over fist while everybody else was bellyaching and moaning that there wasn't an opportunity out there.

Shannon:
Do you have personally a favorite acquisition strategy? Which strategy just makes you the most excited?

Bob:
You know what, I love subject to, but this strategy died during the recession because equity went away and home owners owed more than the property was worth. When I started Renatus, over five years ago, I created a three-hour training series called "Fast Track to Financial Freedom." I showed individuals exactly what was going on in the marketplace, how they could capitalize on what was taking place at that time with real estate investing, and shared with them that we were about 5.2 million homes short of where we needed to be as a nation just to maintain the demand of housing for the increased population.

Many builders do not build in a recession; some went out of business and would need to ramp back up. This would not be an immediate fix. By the time you find raw land, go through all the entitlements, sometimes dealing with the city, and put a foundation in and start putting sticks up to frame the house, you're eighteen to twenty-four months out. It's not like this is just an immediate fix. You don't go, "Oh, there's a demand. I think I'll build a house here." It's going to take a while. I believed that once we got to the backside of the recession, there would be a great housing shortage and that housing shortage would create a massive adjustment in appreciation.

The good news is that the subject to real estate market has come back as prices have increased; we've seen a wild swing. Subject to is a great strategy because it's one of the best ways to acquire multiple properties and not be limited by banks and financial institutions. If you're dependent on conventional lending, you're going to be very, very limited in the amount of real estate you can do and the types of real estate transactions you can do. That's why I love a subject to–it's a great no money down strategy.

Shannon:
What about seller financing? If you're not relying on the banks, are seller financing and subject to the same thing?

Bob:
Well, yes and no. Some might refer to it as another form of seller financing because you are keeping the existing mortgage in place. Generally, seller financing is when a homeowner has a large equity position and they have the ability to create terms for the buyer to make the purchase.

Subject to is when you get the deed to the property, and you become the owner. It's yours. You own it subject to the existing mortgage, but the mortgage still stays in the name of the seller and they stay on the mortgage while you now own and control the home. Now, obviously, you've got to make sure that those payments are made, otherwise the lender will foreclose on the home and even though you're the new owner, they'll take it away from you just like they would have taken it away from the previous owner.

Shannon:
Is a subject to extremely risky as opposed to a standard seller finance, or are they about the same?

Bob:
Oh, no. When we discuss risk we have to think of who's at risk? The seller or the buyer? Individuals looking at selling their home using a subject to' are really in some serious financial stress and they know

that a foreclosure on their credit rating weighs heavier against them than bankruptcy.

Individuals that are stuck in that kind of a situation want to solve that problem before that property goes to auction and the foreclosure is complete. A smart investor will reinstate the loan and purchase the property subject to the existing mortgage. That way, a subject to helps the seller get back on track as far as reestablishing their credit, and it just takes a huge weight off of them. All the stress, all the burden, all the phone calls, all the challenges. It just takes it away so they can get a fresh start and go out and do their thing. The downside for the seller is what happens if the investor who bought the property doesn't make the mortgage payments.

Shannon:
That was my next question.

Bob:
Yep. What happens? Is there a risk? Well, absolutely there's a risk because then that seller could find themselves right back in foreclosure again. Of course, it's no different than the mess they were in to begin with so they're kind of back in the same position. But the bottom line is no investor that is really worth their salt is going to buy a property, put money into that property, and then lose that property because they aren't willing to make the payments. There's a level of assurance that everything's going to happen the way that it should happen.

Now as to the risk to the investor, it's pretty small. Worst case scenario you just walk away from the deal or give it back to the original seller and, if you haven't put any improvements into the property, you're not out anything. If you had put improvements in the property and for some reason you don't have the money to make those monthly mortgage payments, well, then shame on you, you're going to lose the money that you put into the property. Of course, an educated investor would just rent the dang thing out. Then you get a tenant making the mortgage payments for you. There's always a way if you know what you're doing.

Shannon:
That feeds back to all the different strategies. If I, as an investor, were to be in a tough spot and I had learned everything I could learn from you, it seems like I could go to my investment group and say, "Hey, who wants this property? I need help," and they would have the knowledge to help me out.

Bob:
Yep. Absolutely. You know it's just nice to have people that have been there, done that, to be able to pick their brain and lean on them from time to time. We've developed a really unique culture inside of Renatus. It's a culture of servant leadership, meaning that you never, ever ask anybody to do something you wouldn't be willing to do yourself.

If somebody in the community needs help and assistance then we have a pay it forward kind of mentality; but what I see from an awful lot of real estate groups out there, especially a lot of real estate groups, is that they're very motivated to try and maximize their relationships inside the club. There's so many investors in those things that are just looking to prey on brand new investors. They tell them they have a fantastic property that they could turn around and rehab and sell and make 50 grand, but they have to hand over a $10,000 assignment fee to get it.

Then, the brand new greenie goes and buys the property because some seasoned guy said it was going to be a great deal, and they find out that the price they bought it for was over-inflated, the supposed selling price was also over-inflated, and now they're going to lose money on the deal because they didn't know how to work the numbers for themselves. In our community, we apply a lot of emphasis on our leaders and on others in the company to make sure that we take care of community members because they're going to be with us for life.

With that continued emphasis, I outline for them how a deal should be done: Do not sell property to people in the community, unless we want to become a business partner with them, form an LLC with an operating agreement, and have exit strategies already spelled out; do not loan money to anybody in the community or borrow money from anybody in the community unless you become business partners, again with an operating agreement.

That helps to minimize risk. I hate organizations whereby brand new, especially green or naïve individuals get taken advantage of because they think that somebody is trustworthy. You must do your own due diligence because no one is going to care about your financial wellbeing as much as you.

Shannon:

You know, that is so unique to your organization and I love it. If more people just lived their life that way, not just in real estate but just lived their life that way, our world would be so incredibly different.

Bob:

We are all about student outcomes. When somebody buys an educational package from us, after the first year, if they're in good standing with the company, we convert them over to complimentary lifetime access. That means that they're going to have access to refreshed or improved and updated classes given to them for free, for life.

If we have new classes and new material that we roll out to the field, we just give it to our students, again without any additional charge. The complimentary lifetime access is a very, very coveted feature of the Renatus educational system.

Shannon:

You've done a lot of amazing things. You've built businesses, you've adapted, you're married, you have children, you have thousands of people that you mentor and that look up to you every day. What type of legacy to you want to make sure that you leave for them?

Bob:

Let me explain my motivation. The reason why I tick the way I tick, and believe me it's taken a lot of self-evaluation to figure it out, is that when I was a kid I had a father who was an alcoholic and a drug addict. His addictions created an enormous amount of financial stress in the home because we didn't know where our next meal was going to come from or what we would do when the power was turned off. I remember the bishop of our church was kind enough, when we lived behind him, to run an extension cord from his house over to our house so that we could run the refrigerator and watch Saturday morning cartoons after the power and the utilities had been turned off.

There was a lot of financial stress. I was a little kid and I didn't really understand it at that point, but as I started to grow it became more evident. The best thing that ever happened to Dad and the family was when he got caught for check fraud. That's what happens with addicts. They lie, they steal and they cheat, so that they can feed their addiction. Best thing that ever happened to him was he went away to jail for two years. Prison was a forced rehab for him.

When he was sober my Dad was a pretty brilliant guy. He graduated top of his class from University of Pennsylvania, and he went on to get his law degree from there. He was an assistant district attorney in San Francisco and had his own private practice up in Seattle. I mean, he was a smart guy. It was just addiction had taken a toll.

The other thing that meant a lot to me was my church, my faith. I served a two-year mission for my church. I loved every minute of it, being able to teach people how to apply gospel principles to bring them a lot of joy and happiness was rewarding. When you take that kind of philosophy and those correct principles and you put them into business with an investment like real estate, you can teach people a career path that will give them security, stability, financial freedom, and independence. You allow them to then give back to the community and to the world, and you can leave your kids and grandkids a lasting legacy from the inheritance they'll receive when you finally finish your time on this planet.

For me, all of that really has kind of led me to where I'm at today. My greatest satisfaction comes from seeing our students actually do what we teach them how to do and succeed. It comes from seeing them be good stewards of the money that they make. That's another thing, I'm not one of these flashy guys. I've got a nice house and I've got some nice cars, but I'm not driving around in a million-dollar Lamborghini.

There's not a lot of the flash and the bling and the nonsense with me because I don't want to set a bad example for my team. I would rather talk to them about cash flow. I would rather talk about assets. I would rather talk about balance sheets and profit and loss statements and how they can improve their lives and what they're doing to improve the lives of others. If I can make an impact on the community that really transforms their way of thinking so that they act and behave in that manner, we'll change the world.

What brings me the greatest amount of happiness is that I love seeing the positive changes in people's lives. In my first real estate company I dealt with a business partner who lost his focus. His ego got out of hand and he forgot about the people. It was all about his ego and his own self-aggrandizement. His world got so big that he just found himself working harder and harder to feed the monster of his creation. He had an enormous house and expensive cars and private servants and nannies and security details. He even had a jet.

I was just so disappointed with him; he set a bad example for the team. A lot of people in the community wanted to be like him. They started to make really bad financial decisions and leverage themselves into cars and houses and things that weren't producing income for them. He ended up filing for bankruptcy and had to liquidate millions in personal debt.

But life was always good for me because I've always lived well below my means. There's a massive lesson in that. Be a good steward of what you've got, live below your means, and you can still enjoy life, and I do. I enjoy life, and I don't have financial stress, and if everything but my real estate was taken away from me today I would still make a really nice income and never have to worry about money the rest of my life. I want people to have what I have. That's why I do what I do.

Christal Bowlby

Christal Bowlby is the founder and CEO of Christal Clear Visions, LLC and Consumer Financial Solutions. She also acts as a Branch Lending Manager for Geneva Financial, LLC holding personal licenses in the States of Utah and Washington with the company being licensed in twenty-six states. She has over twenty-five years of experience in the real estate and finance industry. As a Realtor, she has earned many Best in Class and Multi-Million Dollar awards and prides herself on customer service and attention to detail.

Even more important than her love for real estate is her passion to help others and make a difference in the world. After hurricane Katrina, she made several volunteer trips to help victims by working with teams to gut and rehab homes while providing love and support to the victims. She has gone on several mission trips to Mexico, China, India, and Nepal, supporting different projects to help the less fortunate. Most of her adult life she has played an active role in programs working with children, the disabled, and the elderly.

Contact Info:

Email: christal@findingsolutions4u.com

Web: www.christalbowlby.com

www.bestparkcityhomeloan.com

Shannon:

What inspired you to get into real estate investing?

Christal:

I actually was inspired many, many years ago. I started in 1990, and I had a friend that had some duplexes. It was very inspiring to me that he had his own successful business. I have always been into design and architecture, and it was fun to go in and see all of the updates and changes that he was making to the property. At that point, I had caught the vision. I saw some of my friends make big chunks of money and be able to work on their own time. That was very appealing and I wanted that too. I've never been one to punch a time clock, so to say. I knew I wanted to be an entrepreneur. That's what inspired me, and it happened an awfully long time ago.

Shannon:

Did you get into real estate right then in 1990?

Christal:

I did, actually. I would follow my friend around because I was trying to teach myself what he was doing. I was young; I was twenty at that point, and he decided to hire me on as his property manager. I started doing some property management work, such as collecting rent, bookkeeping, checking on tenant's issues, and maintaining the property, etc. From that point I thought it would be wise to get my real estate license.

I passed my real estate test in 1991 and worked hard to learn everything I could. I was living in Georgia at the time, and I worked for ERA for about five years. I decided I wanted to learn the lending side, so I talked my way into a position with Chase in 1996 so I could learn all I could about the lending side of things. I've been a lender for about twenty years.   I've done a little bit of everything, and in between I have always invested in rental properties, new builds, or rehabbed and sold properties. It's not always been easy, but I've always enjoyed it.

Shannon:
Since you have started learning in a more formal real estate education forum, how has your investing strategy changed?

Christal:
I'm much more confident. I don't have as much fear built around making decisions on things. Also, I can make a quick judgment call without stressing over it. I can look at something and say this probably isn't really in my wheelhouse and feel comfortable either tackling it, or walking away. There are many types of investment strategies you can follow in real estate, and not all are for me.

Yeah, getting more educated gave me the confidence that I needed. I think in the early days I was just bright eyed and bushy tailed. I was young and wanted to get out there and go after it. I didn't always make the best judgment calls. Even though I had my real estate license, that taught me how to sell real estate not how to invest in it. Some strategies I have learned through the school of hard knocks, some through education, and more through great mentors. It's not always cut and dry; experience and knowledge help to make it easier. I always wanted to ask everyone around me a million questions, but no one person seems to have all the answers. If I surround myself with more than one person, then combined we should be able to answer almost any question out there!

Shannon:
What is your favorite project that you have ever been involved in?

Christal:
When I first moved to Utah, there wasn't much lodging at Solitude Mountain Resort. It was a small family resort. I worked with a developer named Intrawest and the owners of the ski resort to provide financing for the village and condos that were built over several years. We were like a big family; it was a really fun time in my life. I worked mostly with second home and investment borrowers specializing in condos and non-warrantable condo projects. Sometimes we would be hit with a big snow storm, and they would shut the canyon

down for the night so we would all have to stay. Since we were stuck, we'd all get a condo and have a great dinner and play in the snow for the night. It's amazing how quickly you become like family after a few snow storms!

Shannon:
What are some of the creative ways that you use to acquire property?

Christal:
I would say the most creative way is when I work with people who have property in distress. A lot of people don't want to attempt this because it's not easy working with the banks, but I have some advantage with my financing background. I've been able to pick properties up with no money out of my pocket and help homeowners in desperate need of an out. When we went through the mortgage meltdown from about 2008 through 2011, I actually started working with a foreclosure attorney because there were just so many people, past clients, new clients, etc. that were really struggling and losing their homes. The banks were all over the place with a main objective to try to take their homes away without really coming up with a plan that worked for both parties. I learned creative ways to help people that were behind on their mortgage payments and worked with them to either get back on track or move on.

We offer a lot of different strategies regarding foreclosure defense. Sometimes we take the home subject to foreclosure and work with the bank to do forbearance plans or modifications, etc. to help the homeowner until we are able to sell or find a new tenant. I have also done some pretty creative wholesale negotiations where I am able to turn property like that quickly to a new buyer and negotiate some funds from the bank to help the old owner move on. This isn't an easy strategy, but I really love being able to help someone that hasn't been able to resolve their problem, and eliminate some stress from their lives. This strategy can take longer than others and is a pain to work through, but the reward of seeing someone get out of a tough situation is a good payoff. It is also a great strategy to eliminate using a lot of your own funds which makes it lower risk.

In fact, I just sold a house like that where the homeowner was years behind; I worked with the bank to basically secure a forbearance plan. Then we found a buyer while we were still in negotiations, and we were able to turn it quickly using a subject to strategy. The profit was over $37,000, and the homeowner and bank were both very happy with the outcome. The new owner was also able to get it a little under market so it was a win, win for everyone. The owner was so far behind that she would have had to bring in thousands of dollars to bring her loan current; however, the market had increased enough that there was actually equity again. She just couldn't access it because her credit had been ruined, and she owed so much in back payments. The new buyer had cash, so we were able to get an incentive from the bank to close quickly. There was a great profit and all parties were happy.

Shannon:
What is the difference between seller finance and a 'subject to'?

Christal:
This is very confusing. A lot of people assume they are doing seller financing if the seller is offering the new buyer to just pay off the current note, but that should be structured as a 'subject to.' In this scenario, a buyer stays on the current note with the current lender, but you are taking over interest to the property. If a seller offers seller financing, it should be when they have a paid-off note or they have equity that they will secure a new note with terms at the seller's discretion. For instance, let's say a seller owns his property outright and is asking $100,000 (just to simplify things), but the person buying can only secure an 80% loan on that property or $80,000. The buyer doesn't have the 20% difference or $20,000 cash to complete the transaction, but he will have it in the future. He could ask the seller if he would do seller financing for the 20% or $20,000. This means the seller would agree to finance the 20% or $20,000 with agreed upon terms on a new note.

With a 'subject to,' it stays in the original lien holder's name, and the original owner's name will be on the note. If, let's say, I have a loan on my house, and somebody wants to take my property 'subject to' and start paying the mortgage for me. I really am still liable for the note. It can be a touchy situation. You have to know what you're doing, and be careful that you're covering yourself. This is where being very educated about how your contracts are written and having a good real estate attorney behind you are imperative. You should also be fully disclosing how this works to the homeowner and be making sure the lender is okay with it. A lot of people bring up 'due on sale' clauses, and we won't get into all that now, but you shouldn't be doing these types of transactions unless you are familiar with how to protect all parties through well written contracts and have a good understanding of the ins and outs.

Shannon:

Would you recommend doing a 'subject to' with somebody that you don't know?

Christal:

I think if you know what you're doing, if you have the education, and you have an agreement with a well-written contract protecting all parties, then you shouldn't hesitate. I know I have already said it many times, but the key is to be knowledgeable and not just enter into a transaction that you don't understand. Then, yes, it can be a very secure situation, but everything needs to be clear to the person that you're getting into the deal with.

When I do a 'subject to,' it's usually on a property that the person is very motivated to sell. They can't make the payment and then I come in and negotiate with the bank and put myself in control of meeting the terms of the original lender. In other words, when I do a subject to, the person is usually already in a bad situation and struggling to make the payments. At that point, they aren't worried about staying on the note because the alternative could be losing the home anyway. I'm coming in and helping them either get back on track for an equity split down the road, or I'm finding a new buyer to get them out of the situation and possibly some funds to move out.

Shannon:

What is your favorite exit strategy?

Christal:

My favorite exit strategy is when I know I have a buyer before I even enter into the deal, like what they call a wholesale deal. That's an easy, low stress way to do it. There's not usually as much profit as rehabbing and flipping the home yourself, but you don't have as much risk either.

Shannon:
How do you find a buyer before you get into a deal?

Christal:

That takes some time, and it takes building a buyers' list. You can start advertising and networking with other investors to find out what their investor ID or profile is and learn who's really out there doing deals so when you find a good one you can bring it to them and split profits or receive a fee to wholesale it to them. I also have some advantage because I run across people who ask me financing questions, so I find out what they are looking for and if I find something that fits, I contact them. I try to put all prospects in my database so the next time I run across something good, I can let them know and see if I get any bites. It takes time to build a buyers' list, but it's something all investors should be working on if they want to build their network and stay in this business for the long haul.

Then, when you have one that seems to fit their profile, what they like to buy, whether it's multi-family, or residential, etc., you can let them know about your deal which helps you turn deals quicker. That's the best exit strategy I can think of. It's also really important to build a team that you work with regularly and can trust so you don't have delays when trying to exit quickly. Know your own ID: do you like long-term rentals, how long do you want to hold them, or is this something you are flipping quickly? If so, have you studied the market in that particular area? Exit strategies are going to differ a lot depending on the area, market, and type of property.

It may sound cliché, but besides talking to Realtors and appraiser friends about markets, I also look on a lot of the Facebook sites to see what people are looking for. You can find out a lot by the ISO (in search of) comments on some of the 'for sale' or 'for rent' sites. They will ask for three/two or four/two or close to town, etc. This gives me an idea of what people are looking for in the area; then I have to find it and go back and advertise specifically to them.

Shannon:
What is a three/two or four/two?

Christal:
Bedrooms and bathrooms. There are some areas that seem to have a lot of three bedrooms, two-bath homes, or families that may be first-time home buyers that are looking for starter homes, or maybe you are looking in a more established area with larger homes where people advertise that they are downsizing. Once you know what the demand is for that particular market, you know what property to look for.

For example, if you find a lot of people stating they want to down-size, you don't want to put a six-bedroom house under contract in that market because your pool of buyers will be small. Instead, you would look for a smaller, move-down model, such as a three bedroom, two bath home. I find it helpful to sell a home quicker when I know what the demand in the area is.

On the flip side, you wouldn't want to put a three-bedroom, two-bath home under contract in a neighborhood that has growing families or families that already have several kids because it is most likely going to be too small and sit on the market for a long time.

Shannon:
Do you do all of your investing in Utah, or do you do it nationwide?

Christal:
I've invested in other states. I've invested in Washington, Georgia, and California and did a joint venture in Florida. I typically only look at areas that I know well or have done good research on. I'm a little more conservative than some investors and I generally feel more at ease when they are closer to home.

There are some people that will take things right off the Internet and go for it. That's not me, but it works for some people.

Shannon:
Do you think that will ever change for you, and you will take more risks?

Christal:
I do. I'm actually moving that direction where I am increasing the amount of deals I do each year. I was doing more buy and holds in the past, and although that is an important strategy, I learned some valuable lessons from 2008. You need to be able to move with the market and be diversified. Having all long term rentals wasn't a great strategy to have when people were losing their jobs and not able to pay rent. Now, I'm trying to do more flips to have more upfront income along with my long term hold strategy for residual income and equity down the road. I think they're both important.

If you've ever heard the term 'massive and passive,' it makes a lot of sense. Massive would be your upfront bigger returns which can also help you maintain the homes that will give you long term equity or residual monthly income. I think I always knew that before, but I had a tendency to do the buy and hold just because it was easy for me to find renters at the time and not have to work with construction crews, etc. It was an easy way to invest while having another full-time job. I also really like having the extra cash flow. I definitely think the way and where I invest is going to change. It is changing.

Shannon:
Is there anything, when you're looking at a fix and flip home that would keep you from purchasing it?

Christal:
Too much work! Honestly, I am not one that goes for the total ugly, dilapidated homes, that's just me. I'm more the investor that wants to find a good deal with minor cosmetic work that I can get in and out of quickly with less risk verses digging into big overhauls with a lot of potential problems. We've taken down lots of different things, but I wouldn't go for something that was completely falling apart and

really old. I think there's just too much room for bigger cost adjustments that I like to avoid.

I should say it would depend. If there was just so much potential profit room to work with, then I may attempt it, but most of mine just needed minor things and updating. In the market we're in right now, it is getting tougher to find those types of homes, and there are a lot more investors out there looking. It's getting tighter and tighter, so as the market changes I may also need to adjust, but I try to focus on homes that don't have as much room for error.

For example, I was trying to move quickly on a home a while back but I wasn't going to move forward without proper inspections, even though it looked pretty good from the outside and the inside. I did my due diligence and ordered the inspections even though time was of the essence because I knew there were back-up offers and the owner was pushing to give very short inspection periods. Sometimes people want to move too quickly in this market; they just don't bother with inspections because they want to win the contract. It turned out that this property had a big sewer problem, and it would have been another $16,000 to fix. There would have almost been zero profit!

Shannon:
What is the number one piece of advice that anyone has ever given to you when it comes to real estate investing?

Christal:
Know your numbers. I also think right along with knowing how to calculate your numbers correctly is taking the time to get yourself properly educated before you just jump into something just because you've watched some of the guru real estate shows on TV. Real life is different! I see so many people that have the dream. They want to do it. They've maybe replaced a floor in their house or something and now they think they are rehabbing experts. Then they get into a project that's super labor intensive, and it burns them out on their first one. Being educated, and having confidence that you know your strategy well before getting under contract, is key. It eliminates the fear and helps things move smoothly.

Shannon:
Other than education, what advice would you give to someone who really wants to do it but is just afraid?

Christal:
If fear is holding you back, it's probably because lack of experience and knowledge is driving that fear. A lot of people will never make the move on their own because they have never experience it before. My advice would be to get with those that have come before you. Mentorship. Every city has real estate investor groups or clubs (REI groups). Google it and go. The more networking you do with others that are out there doing it, the more comfortable you will become, and you will learn a lot from others. There are tons of different groups online that you can have conversations with via chat, email, meet-up webinars, etc., and ask questions. Get together with some sort of community that have people who are already doing deals and are willing to let you be a fly on the wall, similar to what I did with my friend way back in 1990. It gave me confidence and a passion, and today I am still involved in real estate communities/groups in the area. Elder investors are usually great at giving advice and helping you take those first steps. They may even work with you on a project if you find a good deal. I think you will find that most investors that have been doing investing for a while have support around them instead of trying to be lone rangers.

Shannon:
My last question is: why are you doing this? You have a successful mortgage company. What is different about the legacy that you will leave by doing real estate investing?

Christal:
I want people to admire my drive and the fact that I have made my own way. I persevered even through the darkest times because I never give in and I never give up. I have worked hard to learn this business and help pass that knowledge on to others so that the entrepreneurial spirit can live on. I want people to see my servant's

heart, and know that my love for my friends and family is beyond measure. I have created something from nothing with knowledge and persistence, and I want to pass that on to my nieces and nephew and others. I want to show that you can live on your own terms and do what you love if they choose to create their own destiny and actually believe it to be true. This is my legacy.

Julie Hudetz Dale

Julie approaches every facet of life with enthusiasm and creativity. Her early years in mortgage lending provided a firm foundation for the real estate industry, specifically in the financing component. Meanwhile, her competitive athletic career took her all over the world, as she participated in road races, mountain bike races, adventure races, and triathlons. She even competed with the US National Cycling team and represented the USA at the Winter World Triathlon Championships in Norway in 2006. These two forces of financing and competitiveness have become her strength in real estate investing.

In her first year of investing, she and her husband completed two 'fix and flip' house projects in Denver, and she is currently helping build a community of investors in the Tampa area where she has even more projects in the works. She considers herself the ultimate connector and enjoys bringing people together to work in ways that benefit everyone. She clearly believes in the T.E.A.M. philosophy: "Together Everyone Achieves More."

Based out of Boulder, Colorado, Julie partners with her husband, Scott Dale, who has worked in real estate brokerage and development for thirty-three years. Together, they have built a life that creates positive financial opportunities while leaving plenty of time for fun.

Contact Info:
Email: julie@createawinwin.com
Web: www.createawinwin.com

Shannon:

What inspired you to get into real estate?

Julie:

I have always seen the value in real estate, and it's something that has always appealed to me. It's fun. I always thought I would end up being an agent. I saw the value and enjoy the creative process of real estate. I was motivated by the financial freedom that real estate can provide.

Shannon:

Before you got into real estate investing what were you doing?

Julie:

Before that? Part of my background is that I was a professional cyclist. I raced my bike all over the world. That was a lot of fun, but it didn't pay anything close to what real estate can pay.

After my cycling career, I had various sales, marketing, and training positions in the corporate world prior to quitting my job to focus primarily on real estate. I got tired of the corporate world. I worked fifty plus hours a week, had very little flexibility, and limited earning potential. I didn't have time with my husband. My husband has been in real estate for thirty plus years. He was a custom home-builder and raised by a custom homebuilder, so it's in his blood. We did a big remodel on our home. This is a second marriage, and we wanted a home that we could call our own. We found this great house that was super ugly and nobody wanted to buy it, so we bought it and turned it into something really cool.

During that process we thought, "Gosh, this is fun! We could actually do this together." He's really, really good at the creative side of it. We decided to pursue it together. He currently keeps busy doing commercial real estate; he does commercial real estate brokerage and property management. I'm the one that looks for more fix and flip projects and for opportunities to expand in different markets across the country. We are also beginning to get into private money lending, which allows us to be "the bank." This is a way for us to earn money while also helping other people who want to get started in real estate investing.

Shannon:
Did you end up keeping that home? Or did you end up flipping it?

Julie:
We live in it. We did everything pretty high end because we plan on staying here for a while. We live in a gorgeous home on the golf course. I do not want to leave this house any time soon. It was 80's Liberace marble ugly; it had a baby blue kitchen. It was so disgusting. When we came in, we gave it a new life.

Everybody that drives by our house give us compliments on what a huge transformation we've done to it. Every day I walk in and am reminded of that. I take so much pride in what we've done, what we created together. The long-term investment is huge financially and personally. Gosh, we probably already have a half million dollars of equity in it and it's only been two years! Years before I met my husband, I was in the mortgage industry. I used to work with people that were in foreclosure to help them try to save their homes. I've always enjoyed helping people. In real estate, I like to find win/win situations. If I find somebody in a tough situation that can't pay their mortgage, there are so many creative ways to make it work for everybody, maybe give somebody a chance to start their life over.

I'm definitely a problem solver and always have been. That, combined with the experience and the fun of doing our own remodel, made me realize that this is what I want to do. I have reached a point in my life where it is time to follow my heart. I took a leap from the corporate world, with a secure paycheck, and jumped.

Shannon:
How did that change your life?

Julie:
It was really liberating. I love the freedom and flexibility that we have. My husband, because he works for himself, has always had a lot of flexibility. We love to play, whether it's skiing in the winter, golfing in the summer, getting back on my bike, or just having the flexibility to go to my daughter's soccer game and be a mom. There

is so much freedom in that. I love that I do not have somebody in my office telling me what I can or cannot do.

Shannon:

Do you feel that a successful real estate investment company is dependent on a strong economy?

Julie:

No, not at all. I think that your strategy is going to vary with the economy, but regardless of a good economy or a bad economy, people are going to need a place to live. There's always going to be homes for sale or for rent, so there's always money to be made one way or another, regardless of the economy. You are just going to approach it differently based on what the economy is doing.

Shannon:

What is the best strategy to use when acquiring properties in a rough economy?

Julie:

In a bad economy, the best strategy is to buy rental properties. When home values are declining, it is a great time to buy a house and rent it out. If you have a positive cash flow with a good tenant, you can hold it until the economy turns around and then decide if you want to keep it part of your portfolio or sell it and make a massive return on your original investment.

Shannon:

How important is cash flow in your business? And why should it be one of your primary focuses?

Julie:

Obviously, you have to have cash flow just to survive and pay your monthly bills. How you choose to budget and plan financially is more important. Let's say you have a house that you sell and you make a hundred thousand on it. If you budget your money and plan accordingly, you don't have to have a monthly cash flow because you have that money that you can pull from.

The nice thing about a monthly cash flow is the recurring income that is stable. You've got to think about covering your bills. With real estate investing, you're dealing with a lot of money. Your entire financial strategy has to be considered when approaching deals. If you say, "Hey, I need this buy and hold so I can count on $500 a month coming in" then you're going to need to have a source of money elsewhere. Cash flow is important, but it's the entire strategy of how you manage your money and your finances that is most important.

Shannon:
Do you enjoy doing fixing and flipping or buying and holding more?

Julie:
Initially I am fixing and flipping as many properties as possible so that I can use the money from the fix and flips to build up capital so that I can buy multi-unit properties and keep them as rentals. We live in a college town where multi-unit properties are a solid, long-term investment. In Boulder, Colorado, the housing market is strong. Any type of multi-unit, in the right location, is perfect.

Shannon:
When you say multi-unit, are you referring to duplexes, four-plexes, apartment complexes, or all of the above?

Julie:
Really all of the above; however, I personally don't want to do anything smaller than a four-plex. It comes back to one of the essential sayings in real estate, "location, location, location." If I can get a four-plex across from the University of Colorado, I'll hold on to that forever because I know it will always rent. Then just keep it in good condition. The same would be true for a twelve-plex across from University of Colorado. It's just different factors. What I like about a multi-unit building is that it's all in one location.

Shannon:

Would you purchase a multi-unit property for a little bit more than you think you should, based on the location?

Julie:

Absolutely. Especially since I'm looking at my long-term strategies. If you pay a bit more based on location, you go into the plan to hold it, not flip it for a quick profit. Look at the location and, if you're paying more than you want, you won't want to get out in six months. The strategy is going to be different because you might not recover your money that quickly. If you're looking at a buy and hold strategy you pay a little bit more but you know you're going to keep it for ten years. I would bet on that. Especially in the right location I would bet on the market going up, and I would still make my money over that stretch of time. I would pay more.

Shannon:

If someone were to come to you and say 'Hey, I really want to get started in real estate investing." What would you recommend that they do first?

Julie:

Get educated. Right now. With all the fix and flip reality TV shows, everybody thinks they can be an investor by reading a book or attending a three-day boot camp. People are getting in over their heads without having the right information. Real estate is very profitable. It's also very risky. If you get in over your head or you make one little mistake, even a simple mistake, it can cost you thousands of dollars. If you had taken the time on the front end to get yourself educated and learn, you could avoid those mistakes.

My other piece of advice is to find people that you trust to work with to mentor you and help you in your journey. If you're part of an investor community, it can also help you save a lot of money. I like to use the concept of masterminding on a particular deal. I think it's really good to run your deals by other people, especially if you're just a beginner. It is very important to run the numbers. Let somebody else who has more experience chime in on the opportunity so that they can help determine if it's going to be profitable or not.

Shannon:
Tell me about your most recent mastermind session.

Julie:
A mentor of mine said, "You become the average of the people you associate yourself with." What's so neat about a mastermind group is that as you put yourself around other successful people, it makes you more successful.

Going back to my bike racing career, when I was just starting out my goal was to get on the best cycling team because I knew they would make me a better cyclist. I raced on the number one women's team in the world. Being around that level of talent made me that much better; that's what happens in a mastermind–everybody elevates each other. You have the combination of ideas and strategies and everybody makes more money, accomplishes more. The genuine feeling of satisfaction and accomplishment as a group is a really awesome feeling.

Shannon:
According to Forbes magazine, real estate is one of the top three ways in which people become wealthy. As a real estate expert, why do you feel this is the case?

Julie:
People will always need a place to live. Housing is never going anywhere. Real estate investing is like what we talked about earlier with the changes in economy. People are always going to be buying houses, renting apartments, or renting houses. We're always going to have a need for shelter.

Shannon:
Can everyone invest in real estate?

Julie:
If you're smart. It comes back to knowing what to do and how to do it. People have definitely lost money in real estate over the years. One

of the reasons I think that happens is people perhaps over leverage themselves and then they don't have the resources to sustain the tough economy. If you're going to invest in real estate, yes you can make a lot of money, but you must know what you're doing and have a strategy in place before you do it. People will always, always, be able to make money in real estate. It is not going anywhere.

Shannon:
Other than location, if someone wants to invest in a multi-family dwelling, what is the number one thing they need to know?

Julie:
This applies to houses in any market. You have to know who your prospective buyer or renter is going to be because everything you do should cater to them. If you're in a neighborhood and it's a bunch of young professionals, then you're going to want the finishes and style you choose to appeal to those young professionals. In any strategy you want to think first, "Who is going to live here?"

Take yourself out of the equation. A lot of mistakes new real estate investors make is thinking, "Oh, well if I lived here then _____." You're not going to live there. That's a HUGE part of real estate investing. If you're looking at a multi-unit you might think, "OH, I would never live here." Well, then think about who would live there. Does it matter to that person if you have granite counter tops? Or do you not need to do anything that fancy? How much are you going to be able to charge for rent? You have to calculate how much you're going to be able to make so you don't spend too much on the front end and your numbers still work.

The same thing we're talking about applies to fix and flips. When you do a fix and flip you want to keep it as basic as possible, especially if you know you're going to flip it quickly. There's so many fun and creative things you can do. I don't know if you have been on the site "Houzz," but you can go crazy with super fun, creative ideas, which can be good or bad. Once again, these decisions completely depend on who will be your prospective buyer or renter.

That was one of my mistakes in my first fix and flip. I got too emotionally involved because I love that creative side. We probably got a little more creative than we needed to for who our buyer was. The house was gorgeous when it was done, but we spent more money than we needed to because we got a little too excited about making it really cool. It definitely looked awesome in the end but was probably more than what our eventual buyer needed.

Shannon:
What is a wholesale agent?

Julie:
A wholesale agent is a person who picks up a property at a below-market value and quickly resells it, often to an investor. Let's say they'll find somebody who is a distressed buyer. They work with people who want to get rid of their homes; then they basically just flip it over to an investor and make a wholesale fee. For example, I have a friend who is in foreclosure and she needs to get out of her home quickly and could also use some cash to help her move. A wholesale agent offers a great solution for her. The education part of wholesaling is important. If you don't know what you are doing, it can be disastrous. If you learn how to do it correctly, you can take ownership of that property and sell it to another investor and make what's called a wholesale fee. The wholesale fee ranges anywhere from five to twenty thousand dollars, depending on the property.

Shannon:
Do you use wholesalers in your business?

Julie:
I have used wholesale agents. I would prefer to work within my own community and work with people I know instead of using a whole-sale agent. Personally, that's what I will do on my next fix and flip, or I'll just find the property myself. I'll do the work of a wholesale agent and keep the property, or I might act as the wholesale agent myself, find the property and flip it to one of my investment partners.

Shannon:
What is your five-year plan? Do you plan on still buying local?

Julie:
No, I'm definitely expanding. In fact, I'm currently working on the Tampa area. Bank owned properties are so much more affordable in that community than they are in Boulder. The Boulder market is crazy. The same house that I could buy in Tampa for $200,000 would cost me $600,000 in Boulder.

Shannon:
Do you manage your own properties or do you use a management company?

Julie:
I think you have to evaluate it with your life. If it's not weighing me down, I could manage it myself. My husband, for example, does property management for commercial buildings right now. If you're the one that's on call you're on 24/7, which can be exhausting. The advantage of hiring somebody else to manage the property goes back to the quality of life. I could have more freedom if I hired somebody else to take those calls while I'm off doing whatever I want.

Ideally, I would prefer to hire someone to manage those properties. But if I need to do it myself to make the numbers work I will. It all comes down to cash flow. If the cash flow makes sense and I can hire somebody, that is ideal.

Shannon:
What type of legacy do you want to leave behind? What drives you?

Julie:
My 'why' in my life is my daughter. I got divorced when she was only three years old and raised her as a single mom. I worked like crazy just to pay the bills and take care of her. So, as I get older, I want to be able to leave a legacy of not only the value of property and real estate but showing her that it is possible to follow your dreams and create the reality you want to create; that is the legacy I want to pass on to

her. One thing I've told my daughter since she was little is, "You get to make your own choices in your life. You create your own reality."

I want her to always look at me and think, "My mom followed her heart, worked hard, and achieved what she wanted to achieve." The benefits of that are I will have properties and financial securities that I can pass on to my daughter and grandkids. In everything I do I find myself driven by the motivation of that little girl. That has been the case ever since the day she was born. I am incredibly blessed.

Darren Davis

From jobless to a $3,000,000 profit in five years—all from flipping real estate.

As an eight-year veteran of Real Estate Investing, Darren Davis has completed over 175 real estate transactions in single- and multi-family residences and commercial land development. In 2013, Darren began taking his message across the US as a national instructor to thousands of real estate investor students, and is happy to share his exact business model with individuals. His purpose is to teach others how to create their own success. Darren speaks to hundreds of students on a monthly basis, including audiences in Dallas, Seattle, Chicago, Phoenix, Tucson, Los Angeles, Sacramento, and San Diego.

Darren attributes his success to his tireless pursuit of doing "due diligence" and to knowing his marketplace; he deeply understands that staying on the cutting edge of his industry will provide the greatest value for his students as well as success in his own business. He is passionate about providing hope for others who are looking for a way to exit the "rat race" by helping them grow their monthly active and passive income.

Contact Info:
Email: Darren@Sageinvestingllc.com

Shannon:
What inspired you to get into real estate?

Darren:
The day I got a job was the day I started wondering how long I was going to have to do it before I could retire. I began reading books on how to generate wealth, because I realized my 401K was not going to get me there. I started a program called money mastery, and they encouraged me to read certain books; one book that stood out to me in particular was "Rich Dad Poor Dad" by Robert Kiyosaki.

It gave me a lot of understanding of how wealthy people become wealthy. It didn't tell me specifically how I could become wealthy, of course, but it gave me a lot of good ideas; my interest in real estate was piqued from that point on. It took me another eight years before I actually found a reputable real estate investing education company–one with support group that I could learn from.

Frankly, I tried to do it myself. I pulled a HELOC (Home Equity Line of Credit) on my house. Then I thought I would go buy my first rental, just like I learned in 'Rich Dad Poor Dad'. When I went and looked at houses, I found what I thought might be good investments, but there was just no way of knowing because I was uneducated; because I was uneducated, I was fearful.

Shannon:
How has your education in real estate changed the way that you invest?

Darren:
When I started learning about real estate, the only thing I knew was the whole "buy and hold" strategy. I knew I needed to buy rentals and then collect rent, and hopefully those rents would be more than what I was paying for the property. My business partner and I have now become instructors for the education company that I originally learned from. We are teaching the fix and flip class. I had never taken a fix and flip class before I started doing fix and flips because that was not what I was planning on doing. Fix and flips became a necessity because I needed money sooner rather than later. A good fix and

flip will create a large return on investment in the shortest amount of time. The education made me comfortable with real estate. I saw people of all shapes, sizes, backgrounds, and areas doing real estate, which gave me the confidence that maybe this was not as hard as I was making it out to be.

Shannon:

If somebody that you were talking to was going to get started in real estate, what would you recommend they do first?

Darren:

I often have people say to me "Hey, I want to do what you do. Can I hang out with you?" I reply, "All right, I understand you would like to do what I do, but before you are going to get anywhere, you are going to have to know what I know." I always refer them to the same system that I learned from. Getting some education–you do not have to learn everything–but getting some basic foundational education will give you the best results possible. After they take that first piece of advice I am more than happy to let them "hang out." After all, mentoring people is one of my strengths, and I enjoy doing it.

Shannon:

What is the number one mistake that an individual makes buying their first investment property?

Darren:

The worst thing someone can do is buy a little education–just enough to be dangerous—then go out, borrow someone's money, and try to do this all by themselves. They feel like they are now a "real estate investor," and they want to run before they can walk. My recommendation to people who are just starting out is to partner with someone who has experience. Your chance of success is multiplied 100 times if you have someone by your side who has done it before. I am very passionate about having good partnerships.

The other thing I am passionate about is the belief that you do not have to hit a home run every time. This is not get rich quick. It is get rich, but not get rich quick. Do not try to hit a home run every time, and do not be greedy. There is no reason for that. A base hit is a base hit. There is a reason that people say, "Base hits win the game." A base hit is far easier than hitting a home run. When trying to hit a home run, there are often a lot of strikeouts involved. In this business, you have one bad thing happen to you, and you could be out of business... completely. Small successes, little successes, completing the project and selling it–that is the way to go.

Shannon:
Sticking with your baseball metaphor, is there ever a time when you would want to just have an RBI and take one for the team? Or a sacrifice bunt?

Darren:
Yes, there are times like that. In our business, we base everything on an ROI, or a return on investment. You may be asking $250,000 for a house, and you get an offer for $240K. It might be your first offer, and you are not going to make as much as you want if you take it. But time is money, and if it is going to take me three or four weeks before I get another offer that might only be $10K more, in my opinion it is not worth it.

"Hey look, we are not going to make as much on this one, but we are going to make money. We are going to get out quickly, which helps our return on our investment, and then we can go out and we do another one."

Shannon:
If you are starting with little money or bad credit, what are some strategies that you can use to get into real estate investing?

Darren:
My business partner and I had zero money to our names when we got started. My credit was fair, but his credit score was a 473. We began in 2009 and created our corporation in January of 2010. We had both suffered through the economic downturn. We had no options other

than to do this business without any of our own capital or any of our own credit. Kendall, my business partner, excels at raising money. I suggest that people who have little money or bad credit focus on raising capital from private hard money. It is fantastic because people are generally disconnected from their retirement accounts; it is still their money, but they are disconnected from it because they never look at their statements, and the returns are dismal at best.

When raising capital this way, we are giving people an opportunity to reconnect with their retirement funds. They can direct what is going on with their funds themselves by investing in a tangible, insurable asset like real estate. We are creating a win-win situation where they achieve a good return.

Shannon:

Would you say that real estate investing is dependent on a strong economy?

Darren:

No! In fact, when you are flipping real estate–especially if you are buying at auction or buying houses on the courthouse steps–if you are in a questionable economy, you are going to have a lot more opportunity. When we started buying houses on the courthouse steps in 2009, there was never more than 100 people who could purchase properties that were going up for auction. There just was so much inventory available because we were in a questionable economy; people were unsure if it was going to drop any more or if it was going to start to go up. A lot of people walked away from their houses and lost their jobs. There was a lot of discontent. Because of that, there was an opportunity for others to go in and experience success.

We also had an opportunity to help people with their struggles. If there was no option but for them to lose their house, we could help decrease their pain by giving them some cash to move into rentals or the next place that they are looking to go and create a win-win situation out of what might have been a very uncomfortable situation for somebody. There is no reason someone has to lose in order for you to win. In all of the business we have done, we have been able to do all of it by helping other people. When we are able to buy a house from the bank for cash, we get that off of their books, and they get to use that money for another investment. We may have to do an "eviction" on the house because someone might be living in it, but we talk to them like they are people. We work with them, and we offer them a cash settlement–even though they have lost their house because they did not make their payments–so they can carry on with dignity.

We go in and fix up a house that may have deferred maintenance on it because its residents were undergoing financial hardship. We sell it for top of the market at the time, creating a rising tide for the whole neighborhood. A nice family moves in. In this area, it is usually a military family, because they are able to fairly easily obtain financing. They were the last few who could, so we are getting young families into these houses and creating a better neighborhood. Nobody loses. If someone had a problem, we are able to lessen the sting of that in some way and help them out. We have had people that we have "evicted" who have given us glowing recommendation letters for our business.

Shannon:
What have you done to make it through rough times in your real estate investing?

Darren:
No matter how successful someone appears, they all have their own struggles. The struggles that we have in our own real estate business are all able to be conquered. My uncle was selling his condo and getting into an apartment. He was running into some struggles with the apartment management company and was not sure that they were going to be able to qualify him.

It was nice to be able to say, "Hey John, you know what, we'll get this figured out. That's no problem. It's an easy problem to take care of. We've got a couple of different options."

We started a business on nothing but huge load debt. We have been able to make it from day to day, month to month, and year to year by just doing what we do and continuing to stay on that path. We create those base hits every chance we get. For us, attitude is everything.

Shannon:

You are a very successful real estate investor with over 180 homes purchased. What do you think it takes in the real estate world to be a good leader?

Darren:

A good leader leads by example. I do not ask people to do things I am not willing to do. Good leaders are truthful and real; they do not put on a façade that they are better than anyone else. People see right through that. Good leaders are able to get down in the trench, roll up their sleeves, and work side by side with those they are leading; they do not lead from the office chair from afar while everyone else is out digging ditches. I like being real—being real with people and letting them know that, "Hey, we are all in this together." Just be real. People like you better that way. They may not agree with what you are saying, but they will respect you more.

Shannon:

How do you define success?

Darren:

Success is defined so differently by so many people. I have in my office a wall of fame. It is thirty-four 8 1/2 x 11 frames up on the wall, each of them deals we have done. They are not all the best ones; in fact, we have our worst one up there as well. But there are some of the average ones, some of the good ones–just a whole bunch of deals that we have done so people can see that a picture of the house, the address, how much profit was made, the return on investment for our investors, and how many days it took us.

The worst deal on the wall was one which took us five months to complete on a $200,000 investment, netting us $121.00!

The $121.00 had to be split four ways. Some people would not consider that a success. In my book, I see it as a success. We got in, we fixed it up, and we did everything right. We just had problems with the property that were unexpected, and it ate up all of our profits almost to the penny. What we did not do is give up on it, throw in the towel, or go negative. We persevered. To me, that is a success. If you can get through your first project and do better than breakeven, that is a success.

Sometimes your success may even cost you some money, but teaches you some lessons. If there is a project out there that you have learned anything from, then I would consider that a success.

Shannon:

When doing a fix and flip, what do you look out for and what do you think is the best strategy for finding fix and flips?

Darren:

When looking at a fix and flip I look for three things:
1. What is it worth?
2. What am I going to be into it for including my profit?
3. What can I get it for?

I always start with the end in mind and reverse engineer it. If one of those things goes awry, then what do I need to do in order to massage that or change it up a little bit so that we can still come out with a profit.

Shannon:

Other than price, what would be one of the things that would make you walk away from a fix and flip?

Darren:

Price fixes the majority of problems. If the neighborhood is kind of downtrodden, you can still make a nice property and sell if for less, and someone is going to be happy with that. The only other thing that would really deter me from purchasing a house besides price would be who I have to deal with in order to make a deal happen. If someone brings me a property or has a problem or are looking to sell their property, but they are difficult people to deal with, I choose not to deal with that kind of person. If I can see that the person I am dealing with does not seem to be very honest or if something feels off, then I am probably going to look somewhere else for that deal.

Trust your gut feeling. If it does not feel right, there is a reason why your gut is telling you it does not feel right. The more you trust it, the easier it will become to understand why your gut is telling you what it is.

Shannon:
Do you have a favorite fix and flip, and why?

Darren:
The ones that stand out to me are the ones where actually we have been able to go in. For example, I am meeting with a lady today out in Mission Viejo. She has a house that is in disrepair, and her husband recently passed away. She is now the sole income provider for her household. Her adult daughter has been living with her, but has some challenges of her own, which has created chaos in the house. The lady has been unable to pay consistently both her mortgage and the HOA, which is just creating drama in her life. She has a good job, but there are a lot of medical bills, and she has fallen behind.

This deal was brought to us by an agent who is listing the house for the woman, but it is coming down to the wire. Even though she has equity of $150,000 to $170,000 in the house, she may lose everything because it has been in default for too long. What we have been able to do is go to her and let her know that, "Hey, look. We can stop all of this. We can take this away from you; take this burden off of you by paying off the HOA, catching up the mortgage, doing the repairs on the house and then selling it for a higher price. We can do all that. Keep the foreclosure off your record, keep the eviction off your record. We can do that and give you $30,000."

When she heard that, she was ecstatic because she was living in fear in her own home because she doesn't know when or if the sheriff would come and evict her. It could have happened at any time, but we were able to step in and help; we did not just give her money to help her along, but we actually saved her credit and her ability to be able to take care of herself. We all struggle in different ways, and we do not know what is going on and sometimes we just reach out a little bit. There are people out there who we can help. Instead of having nothing and living in fear, she is going to walk away with enough money to put a down payment on a new house, a clean credit record, and peace of mind.

Shannon:

What kind of legacy do you want to leave behind?

Darren:

A lot of people, when they think of leaving behind...sorry, it is an emotional topic for me.

When most people think of leaving behind a legacy, it has to do with leaving behind a lot of money or a big inheritance, but the legacy I want to leave for my children is that I want them to know that there is nothing that they cannot get through; that no matter what life throws their way, it is okay, and that there is always someone else out there who has been through it. With a little bit of hard work, some tenacity, and an unyielding desire, they can accomplish whatever it is that they set out to do.

Nate Lambert

Nate Lambert is the proud father of four boys. He was a family psychology professor and the author of over 65 research articles and book chapters on the topic of thriving in life. He also served as an editor and presented his research across the United States and on 4 continents. Dr. Lambert is also the author of the book *See the World on Any Budget,* as well as the books *Publish and Prosper, Standing Up for Standing Out: Making the Most of Being Different,* and *Four Truths about Weight Loss that Nobody Tells You.* He also finds time to write articles for *Psychology Today*! He loves international travel and recently lived with his family in Fiji for 7 months. But now, he focuses exclusively on real estate as a Realtor and a professional investor. He currently owns multiple rentals and has done fix and flips that have netted him six figures in profit. Using his experience, knowledge, and skills, he actively coaches dozens of investors on how to build their own successful real estate business.

Contact Info:
Email: natemlambert@gmail.com

Shannon:

What made you decide to be a professor? Do you think that was what you really wanted to do or was it just what was expected of you?

Nate:

I have a great love of learning, I've always been into reading and self-development, and I love public speaking. I thought of being a professor as a way to gain the credibility to be a speaker and travel the world and also to write things that influence people. That's what I got into it for, but then I realized that very few people actually read the stuff that most professors write. It's hard to really make much of an impact. However, I did write some books that have had an impact, and my journal articles are constantly getting cited by other scholars. I don't regret going that route. It was very enriching. The experiences I've had are very rewarding.

I was even a professor in Fiji. I've lived around the country and traveled everywhere for conferences. That experience was incredibly enriching, so I'm glad I did it. In fact, I'm using a lot of those skills I developed: the writing and thinking and organizing and team building, mentoring, and teaching. I'm teaching almost more now than I did as a professor. I'm actually utilizing a lot of those skills I developed as a professor and carrying them over into real estate. I think that's partly why I'm succeeding at a high level in real estate, because of those things. Although the professor experience added a lot to my life, I'm really glad that I found my true niche now as a real estate entrepreneur.

Shannon:

It is amazing how we, as people, all get our inspiration from different areas. Is it fair to say that your love of learning inspired you to get into real estate?

Nate:

Well, it was actually while I was still in graduate school. At the time, I was learning how to publish, and I learned it really well. I actually published 7 books and almost 70 journal articles. I was an editor of a renowned journal. However, I was getting really bored. How many times do people curl up behind the fireplace and read a journal article? Few people outside of academia read or care about those things. I just felt like I really wasn't making any real world impact.

I was just looking to spice things up a little. I had a friend of mine, actually a graduate student, who gave me a book about real estate. His dad had started investing in real estate. But I had never really seriously considered investing because my parents had a bad experience with it. When my friend gave me this book, I'm like, "No, that's okay." I put him off, and then five or six months later, I was listening to all these taped programs about how to become rich, because I thought, "That's a cool goal to pursue to give me something to do in all my spare time as a bored professor." When I caught up with my friend again, I realized, all these books were saying the same thing, they said, "Real estate, real estate, real estate. This is the biggest path to wealth. This is the most common way to get there." It kind of softened me up.

And then when I was visiting Florida, where I got my PhD, and I was staying at my friend's house. His name is Preston. I was listening to this seminar while I was at his house, about becoming wealthy, and he stopped me and said, "You know what, you really should think about real estate." He was persistent with me. He gave me the book, and I read the entire thing on the plane ride home. I was just fascinated by it. It just really grabbed me, really spoke to me, like nothing else had to that point. That's kind of what got me, was seeing the vision. The author really painted a powerful vision of the financial freedom that real estate can bring, and that really attracted me.

Shannon:
What was the best piece of advice you took from that book?

Nate:
The strategy they advocate in that book is to buy single family homes, because they say that those are the most reliable. They're the safest kind of investment. Then you should lease option them out to a renter. That way you get a down payment, you get higher rent,

and you get a renter who takes care of the property since they have a greater financial stake in it. I guess in some ways, it also introduced me to some aspects of creative financing.

Shannon:

Do you follow that strategy? Do you think that the lease option is the best path for real estate success?

Nate:

Yes. For me, it is. I've learned more and more, that book kind of got me started. I learned through joining an investor community, more about seller financing, which is similar to a lease option.

Seller financing has been my primary focus as an investor, because you can acquire properties without using a bank. Other people or programs teach you to buy properties through a bank, and so I actually acquired my first property through a bank. I had to put $38,000 as a down payment, and I was able to buy that property through a home equity line of credit I got on my personal residence. However, I wanted to go faster, and I wanted to figure out how to do this more myself. I started connecting with local investors, and I learned the strategy of seller financing. In fact, I mentored with a guy that has 250 properties that none of which are through a bank. That was super inspiring to me because I wanted to have a huge portfolio like that, and I knew that I couldn't do that through a bank.

I knew that I didn't want to be putting $40,000 down for every house that I bought. I needed a quicker route. I've made seller financing my primary area that I specialize in because I believe in having a large portfolio and getting that cash flow coming in every month. That's the best possible retirement plan. To do that, you've got to acquire them creatively, in my opinion. Seller financing is a great way to do that. I recently acquired a property in Kearns, UT that they've agreed to give a $12,000 down payment, so that covers a lot of the cost I had to put out to buy the property. Then if they default, if they can't execute their options, I get to keep that option payment. I get to keep their option, just like the bank would. The bank's not going to give you your down payment back if you foreclose, if you can't make the payments.

That's the cool thing about seller financing or a lease option; you become the bank. You get to keep someone's down payment, and then you can put someone else in there as another lease option. The main downside about the lease option is that you often will lose the property because someone will execute their option and then they buy it. That's not necessarily a good thing if you've spent a lot of time acquiring the property, and you've found a great deal, and then you actually lose the property when they buy it through a lease option. That's the main downside of doing the lease option. One of the reasons I lean more toward seller financing than lease options is that you're buying a home without using your own credit. Usually, you do need to put some money as a down payment or maybe to catch them up on their payments if they're going through foreclosure.

Let me tell you about the most recent deal I did with seller financing; that will help illustrate this. My partners and I approached someone that was in pre-foreclosure, and said, "Hey, you're in a bad situation. How far behind are you in your payments?"

They said, "Oh we're $6300 behind."

"Okay, well what if I were able to get you caught up, would that help you out?"

"Absolutely. That would save our credit. That would save us from being foreclosed on!" That's a win for them.

"Where are you going next? Because obviously if I buy this house from you, you can't stay in the house because I need to rent it out. Where would you like to go next?"

"Oh, we'd love to go to Cedar City."

"Okay, great. What do you need to get to Cedar City?"

"Well, we need a motorhome to drive our stuff and a place to live, in this motor home."

I think they had some relatives that owned some land they could just live in their motorhome on the property.

"Great. How much could you get an inexpensive motor home for?"

"$7000." "Okay, tell you what... what if I caught you up with Wells Fargo—I'll cut a $6300 check to Wells Fargo—and then I'll get you on your way. I'll give you $7000. I'll give you $5000 up front, then I'll give you another $2000 when you're out of the house and give me the keys..."

You've always got to keep that leverage over them, to make sure that they actually leave and don't try and squat on their own property.

"...and you can be on your merry way, go get your motor home, go to Cedar City. Is that a win for you guys?"

"Absolutely."

Shannon, is that a win for Wells Fargo?

Shannon:
Absolutely?

Nate:
Absolutely it is.

Now they're getting their payments. They don't have to go through the expensive foreclosure process and auction this off at a discount. They're getting paid by me. These people are still on the mortgage, and frankly, for the next 28 years, I'm going to be paying on their behalf. Not only is their credit saved from the foreclosure, but they're going to continually increase their credit because now I'm making the payment on their behalf. The mortgage does stay in the seller's name, so if the seller needs to buy a new property immediately, it's not the ideal option for them, because it's going to count against their debt to income ratio. But in this situation, it's a win for them. After a year, 100% of my payment counts towards their income. Essentially, they could go buy a new property, and it's not going to count against their debt to income ratio.

Shannon:
Does the bank worry that the owner is no longer occupying the property?

Nate:
This is a fully legal process, and the banks are aware it's happening because it's a well documented process. Ultimately, it's better for them because they have two people now that are on the hook. If I, as the investor, stop making the payments, then the other person is on the hook for that. In a lot of ways, it increases the chances that

they're going to get paid. Most banks are like, "Hey, if we're getting our payment, it doesn't really matter who it's coming from. We're getting our payment." There is a small chance that there is what's called "a due on sale clause." My mentor that I told you about earlier has 250 properties. He has never had a bank call the note due.

In terms of the benefit to me, now I had a property. My payment was about $1000 a month, and I rented it out to these people on the lease option for $1600. They were paying a little more than market rent because I was giving them the option. I'm making $600 a month in cash flow on this property, and I had about $30,000 that I picked up in equity. I'm going to profit about $39,000 when this sale goes through. I like to structure all my deals so that it's a win either way. If they buy the property, I pocket $39,000. If they don't, I pocket $12,000 and can move on to the next person. I'm really pretty happy with whatever happens in this scenario. It's always smart, as an investor, to consider all your exit strategies before you do the deal. You've got to make sure that, regardless of the scenario that occurs, you're covering your bases, and you're going to profit regardless of what specific thing happens.

Shannon:
Do you ever keep people as a tenant just paying rent versus doing a lease option?

Nate:
Yeah, absolutely. Everything's negotiable. As long as you have plenty of options in front of you, everything's negotiable.

Shannon:
When you enter into an investment property, how many exit strategies do you recommend people have?

Nate:
I usually suggest at least three. You want to have, "Here's my most desired exit strategy." If you're doing a fix and flip, for example, maybe you're like, "First of all, I don't want to sell, but what happens if the market goes down while you've been fixing and flipping this

property for 3 or 4 months? Property values are starting to fall sharply. You want to say, "If that happens, or if I can't get a decent price and I'm going to potentially rent this house, or put it up as a seller finance or a lease option... You always want to have option A, but then also have B and C ready to go, so regardless of what happens in the economy, you can always make a profit and make it work. You want to hedge your bets as a smart investor; you want to set things up so that you can win regardless of external circumstances.

Shannon:

Is it your opinion that real estate investing is not dependent on a strong economy?

Nate:

It is absolutely not. In fact, I've started a wholesaling business with a partner who has 31 properties. He's worth over 2 million. He bought a number of properties during the huge economic downturn in 2008 and 2009. He's told me several times: his biggest regret is that he didn't buy more. A great example is, do you buy Valentine's Day candy on the 13th and 14th of February or on the 15th?

Shannon:

The 15th.

Nate:

Yeah, the 15th, that's when everything goes on sale! This partner, he has these focus groups with the leadership of the local areas here in Utah, and he's noticing that a lot of the top investors right now, in Utah, are hoarding their cash. They're not wanting to buy properties as much right now because everything's so expensive. Utah is one of the hottest markets in the country! In some opinions, this isn't a good time to buy. A lot of these guys are waiting for everything to go on sale during the downturn which creates a great opportunity for wholesaling. Ultimately, if you have the right knowledge, and you apply the right strategies at the right times, you can make money in any economy.

Shannon:

*What is one piece of advice you would give to someone who is just begin-
ning their journey in Real Estate Investing?*

Nate:

You've got to be flexible. You've got to see what the trends are and
what's going on, yet have enough knowledge about different strategies that you can just switch gears and take advantage of the new
circumstances. Everyone right now is thinking, "Oh this is the best
time. Real estate's so hot right now." In actuality, for a lot of investors, this is a hard time, because there's so many competing investors there right now since everything's so hot. The margins are
definitely slimmer. Auctions—you almost can't even get a good deal
right now. Ironically, it's almost a harder time to be an investor right
now, whereas, during the down times, it's like, "Oh baby." Tim and
I, our strategy is that we're going to be ready with a wheelbarrow to
go around and just pick these properties up when we have another
downturn. We're just waiting with a lot of excited anticipation for
the downturn. Obviously, we don't ever like to see anyone lose their
job or bad things happen, but in terms of our business, this is a great
time to get in.

In fact, Warren Buffett always said, "Be fearful when others are
greedy and greedy when others are fearful." The idea is that when
people are getting greedy right now, this is the time to maybe hold
back. When people fear, that's the time to get greedy because that's
the time when you're going to get everything on discount. Ultimately,
you want to have that kind of strategy in mind. You've just got to
have enough knowledge and have enough tools in your tool belt, so
you can make it in any economy. You've got to be flexible and be
willing to switch gears.

Shannon:

*Since you believe that it's harder to buy in Utah right now, are you in-
vesting in other areas of the nation?*

Nate:

I am.

We don't have the deal closed yet, but we're looking at getting 96 properties for just over $700,000 in Illinois. These properties, they're very inexpensive, but will have a lot of deferred maintenance The plan is to divide them up to fix them and do a flip that we will do ourselves. We're going to be able to sell these houses for $5000 or $6000 down on seller financing. $30,000 to $35,000 a pop to own a house free and clear. For people here in Utah, that's like, "Wow. That is cheap." If all of the numbers work out, and it goes through as planned, I'll make a 21% return over the next year.

Shannon:

What is wholesaling, and how do you make money doing that?

Nate:

I started a wholesaling company, Property Solutions Team. We look for properties that we can pick up at a discount. We're really trying to pick up most of these through seller financing. We convince people that they want to sell the property to us, and we'll make payments to them on seller financing. Then what we do, maybe we get the property locked up for, let's say, a $5000 down payment, for example. We pay the seller $5000, and we get it under contract. We don't actually purchase the property ourselves; Tim and I both have hundreds of real estate investor contacts we've developed by going to local club meetings for the last few years.

We go and approach these investors and say, "Tell you what, how would you like a house on seller financing?" Which everybody wants one of those because they're not easy to find. All these investors don't want to use their own credit to make the deals go. Everyone wants those and we say, "Look, I've got this house for 28 years using their mortgage. I will sell it to you for a $20,000 down payment. Are you interested?" A lot of people will say, "Absolutely. Sign me up." We make the $15,000 difference. That's what's called a wholesale fee. We negotiate the deal and get it under contract before we've actually purchased the contract. We pass the contract on to another investor who loves the deal. In the contract we put, this is for us or assigned, whoever we assign to the contract. The seller understands that there's a chance we may not be the end buyer. We let them know that. Investor Joe says, "Yeah I want that, so I'll pay $20,000." Without even having to put our name or do any closing costs or anything, we've just pocketed $15,000 without any liability, without any risk.

If we can't find investor Joe, then we say, "Mr. Seller, Bob, I'm sorry, but we've decided we don't really want to buy your property after all." Obviously, we try not to do this because that doesn't make Seller Bob happy, but it doesn't really harm him. He still can sell it. That happens all the time in real estate: people come and get a house under contract, and they're not able to buy. So they turn it back over to the seller and they sell it to someone else. No harm, no foul.

Shannon:
Do you lose that $5000 you gave to Seller Bob, if it falls through?

Nate:
We never gave Seller Bob any money. We might have given a title company $100 of earnest money, but ultimately, in the contract we wrote out that we have 15 or 30 days to do inspections and ultimately, you can get out of that contract. In the state of Utah at least, the buyer can get out of about anything. As long as we don't extend beyond our 30 days of due diligence time, we can get out of that without paying Seller Bob anything. We don't even have to pay him the earnest money. Let's say Investor Joe comes along: we pass it on to him, and he executes the contract. Now Seller Bob gets his $5000 we agreed to, and he's happy. We get our $15,000, and we're happy. And Investor Joe is super happy because he got a house he wasn't able to find on his own, and for a decent deal, with seller financed terms. Everybody wins. Everybody's happy.

Wholesaling is absolutely the lowest risk kind of investment that you can make. A lot of people think, "Oh that's easy." No, actually, it's not, because you have to get good at finding deals, and you have to get good at selling the deals to other people. There's a lot of steps involved, but especially in a market like we have right now, that's so hot, we don't necessarily want to get these properties ourselves because maybe they're a little overpriced right now. We would rather just keep that $15,000 and store it up for when everything goes on discount on February 15th, when the market corrects or crashes. We're going to go around with our wheelbarrow, picking them up.

Shannon:
When you start to teach and mentor other investors, do you feel like you end up competing with those same people?

Nate:
You definitely are competing with people, but I really like to have an abundant mindset. There's the scarcity mentality, and then there's abundant mentality. The scarcity folks are out there, they're not sharing any of their secrets, and they're not sharing any of their strategies. They're always thinking that there's a shortage. I like to have an abundance mindset where; I'm going to help other people. I'm coaching dozens of people and teaching other investors on how to do what I'm doing because I really believe that there's a lot of deals out there. And a lot of deals aren't getting found; they aren't getting done. There's enough pie out there for everyone, in my opinion, so we need to help each other.

There are a lot of deals, and people who have the scarcity mindset tend to always think, "Oh, there's nothing out there." If you feel that way, it's going to be motivating for you to go out and look. Whereas, if you have an abundance mindset, even for me, as I've told you, it is a little tighter market right now because everything's so hot. But I still try and maintain an abundance mindset where I'm like, "There's plenty of deals. We'll go find them." I am finding them. That's my perspective on that.

Shannon:
What's the most creative way that you've come up with so far to find these properties?

Nate:

What I'm doing right now is having this wholesale business, so it's not just me and my partner. I've now got 15 to 20 people that are out looking for deals for me. They're calling and pounding the pavement. They're calling people off of the classifieds, searching for vacant properties, and so on. We all share in the profit when the deal clears.

Shannon:

Do they get a bonus when they sign a property?

Nate:

Yeah. They get a bonus, so they're more motivated. I can just spend my time analyzing the deals they're bringing to me. We're just getting started, but it's working great.

Shannon:

You shared that you're mentoring several people right now. Do you still keep in contact with your mentors?

Nate:

Yeah, absolutely. I have a mentor, and we speak regularly. We just talked about a business idea I had yesterday, and he helped me to think through that carefully. Being a professor, at one point I had as many as 30 students working for me. I was mentoring them, and they were helping me. It's a collaborative situation that benefits everybody. A lot of people think, "I can just do real estate on my own. I can read some books, find some kind of webinar online, and I can do this myself." As a professor, I would liken that to someone saying, "Oh yeah, I'm just going to read some books on psychology, and I'm going to write a journal article and publish it in a great journal." That's just not possible because it's all about mentoring in this business. It's a relationship business, and there's a lot of steps to this business you can't just teach yourself. Obviously, reading a book, like I did, is a good way to kind of get interested and get started, but ultimately, you need a mentor.

Just like a professor takes someone under their wing and helps them to learn how to write a literature review, and how to design a study, how to write it up, and publish the results. It's a back and forth process, and it's a complicated process. Everybody involved and myself as a professor—we all win because when we publish, they get their name on the publication, I didn't have to do a lot of the legwork, and I get my name on the publication. Honestly, it's the same thing in real estate. You mentor once you know more and have more expertise. You can be that mentor, and you can have other people on your team, like I do with Property Solutions Team. You're teaching and training them, and you're showing them what to do. They're learning; everyone's benefiting.

They're becoming investors, and I'm not having to do a lot of the legwork. Instead I'm focusing on my area of expertise and really trying to help them analyze, and I'm training them and helping them. Everyone wins when you have a mentor. This mentorship model is what all successful businessmen, or women, do, what professors do. It works just the same in real estate. You've just got to have the education, but you also have to have a mentor to help direct you and know how to take action to put you in a profitable situation

Shannon:
How has real estate changed your life?

Nate:
I went from kind of being a bored professor to something exciting, and really, I've always been an entrepreneur, so I think even though I was very successful as a professor, that wasn't the right role for me. What real estate's really done for me is just allowed me to really find self-expression and to really find so much passion. There's so many times when I'll stay up after a meeting and not be able to get sleep till midnight. I'll wake up at 4 just excited to get started and think of new, creative ways to do this business. It's just unleashed my creativity and given me so many outlets to connect with amazing people. It's given me so much excitement in my life. It's not just about the finances; it's powerfully changed my life. First, financially, but also to develop the relationships that I've developed. You'll have this passion while seeing your ideas come to fruition, and helping other people has just been such a thrill of a lifetime. I'm so grateful that I made this switch.

Shannon:
What kind of legacy do you want to leave behind?

Nate:
Ultimately, the legacy I want to leave is to create millionaires. I want to create people who know how to generate wealth and can teach and train others. My vision is to help hundreds of people to achieve financial freedom in their lives. I want to help them to see that they need to actually do amazing philanthropic things with that money. I feel like by me helping and mentoring these other people, I can not only help them to become millionaires, but I can help them to teach others to achieve financial abundance and freedom and to do great things with that money that will help and bless the world.

For myself personally, I've already been traveling the world with my family. I've been to over 30 countries on 6 continents. We aren't waiting until we're millionaires or wealthy, filthy rich people. We lived 7 months in Fiji because of our real estate wealth that we created. We moved to Fiji for 7 months and had a grand adventure, an amazing experience. I'm living my dream right now. I'm taking my wife to the Dominican Republic in August. We're planning on going to Thailand for Christmas. Just traveling the world with my family and creating these amazing memories and having these cultural experiences—that's what really drives me as an individual.

Just start living your dream now. I've written a book called See the World on Any Budget. I even did that before I started achieving real estate wealth. For me, I just want to live my dream now, and real estate gives me the best possible way to get the time freedom—and the money freedom—to do what I want to do in life. That's really exciting.

Susa Lindsey

Susa Lindsey earned her Master's degree in Deaf Education from Utah State University in 2007. For ten years she taught preschool to seniors in high school. Her passion for working with learners with special needs gave her great joy, particularly as she watched her students discover and understand new and complex topics. Every day she felt blessed to witness these amazing kids develop as independent caring individuals.

Working with young adults strengthened Susa's belief that every person has a unique talent and can elevate the world around them. She continues her mentorship with adults who are looking for financial independence through business ownership and real estate investing.

The business world is always changing and investing offers many opportunities for dynamic growth, whether a person has several properties or is looking to buy their first property. Susa sees the same excitement in the faces of new investors that she saw in her past students.

She enjoys building new relationships and strengthening old ones as she helps people gain a better understanding of the market and how to use it to create win/win opportunities for everyone while elevating the community.

Contact Info:
Email: yourinvestingmatrix@gmail.com

Shannon:

According to Forbes magazine, real estate is one of the top three industries in which people become wealthy. As a real estate expert, would you agree?

Susa:

I completely agree that real estate is one of the best ways to gain wealth. What one thing does everybody need? Everybody needs a place to live. We all need a roof over our heads. But that's not all. Everybody is also looking to improve upon what they already have, an even better place to live. There's that pressure to keep up with the Jones', and real estate fills that need. For some people, the bigger, the better. For others it's a cute little bungalow tucked away in the everglades. Real estate is very personal; it can be exactly what you want it to be, and it lets you chase your dreams.

Real estate investment gives people many different options for earning. You can help yourself as well as other people. And the more you help others, the more money you make. It's wonderful.

Shannon:

What inspired you personally to get into real estate?

Susa:

I'm a teacher by trade. I work with the deaf and hard of hearing. I enjoy teaching and watching kids learn new things. But the unstable economic and political conditions have affected everything, from education to the stock market, which is where I'd hoped to build my retirement. I was looking at my 401K and thinking, oh, that's a 101K! I'll never reach the financial goals I'd hoped for by the age of 65. I'm not where I need to be now, let alone when I retire. And if things continue trending this way I worry my 101k will end up a 1k. Thinking about all that made me realize I needed something more, something I could count on. So I started looking into how I could supplement my income and, eventually, replace my income. Real estate seemed like the best way to reach my goals.

As a real estate professional I can make a passive or active income. An example of a passive income would be earning on rent, whether it's from a commercial businesses or a single-family home. I can use that to make money to supplement my income, plan my retirement and enjoy a certain lifestyle. I can also renovate a house and add value to the neighborhood and community, as well as to the house itself. I can make from $20,000 to $50,000 or more by selling that house after it's been fixed up. I looked at my life and decided I wanted more of passive, and massive, income.

Shannon:
When you look at your life, do you see yourself leaning more towards commercial or residential?

Susa:
I enjoy the residential side because I'm able to help more people directly. Commercial real estate is also important because we all need different things to live and survive. And it's a great endeavor for some people. I like to work with those who need help to get going in life and who are ready to work differently for it. Maybe their job is not paying what they need exactly at that moment and I enjoy helping them by putting a roof over their heads so that they don't have to worry about that part. They can worry about bettering their life. They can also take control of their life.

Shannon:
It sounds to me like that's one of your passions, perhaps since you are a teacher for the deaf and hard of hearing. Right away you decided that if you were going do something else you wanted to be sure that it would make a difference in other people's lives as well as your own. You're doing something right. Good job.

Susa:
Thank you. I am very passionate about that because everybody deserves to be given the opportunity to better their lives. Not everybody may take the opportunity, but everybody deserves it.

Shannon:

If somebody came to you and wanted to start in real estate investing, what would you recommend they do first?

Susa:

Talk to people. Work with the people I work with and grow your network. The people in my network can answer your questions. Real estate is part of an ever-changing and dynamic environment; if you have information that is just six months out of date you could lose thousands of dollars. I don't want that to happen to anybody. Building a trusted network is key—get to know a title guy, loan officer, great and honest contractors. Start talking to people. Ask questions.

Shannon:

It sounds to me like you are big on teams. Do you think that people can go into real estate investing alone and be successful?

Susa:

It's risky. There are people that do it short-term because they found a fantastic opportunity and deal of the year. Then they'll go into another deal thinking they know everything and end up making a mistake. It's not easy to go at it alone. You need a lot of resources like the few I mentioned earlier and a lot more on top of that. You can't be an expert at everything and you shouldn't even try.

Shannon:

Let's say a general contractor wanted to get into real estate, would you recommend that they do it all themselves or would you recommend they hire someone?

Susa:

That would depend on their goals and skill set. If they want maximum control and can handle it all themselves then I would totally support them. But I would also remind them that it's a slow process, especially for fix and flips because you can only be at one location a time. Whereas if you contract some of the work, and are good at managing people, you can handle anywhere from two to six locations at any given time. And once you start managing people, rather than locations, you can get a lot more accomplished and help more people and the community.

Shannon:
When you're doing a fix and flip, what are some of the things that you look for?

Susa:
I look at the foundation to be sure there's no structural issues. If structural issues do exist, I may not be able to recuperate the reno-vation costs. It's not worth my time unless the renovation costs are covered and I have a sufficient profit margin. The second thing I check is the roof—does it leak or need to be replaced? Plus, I always use quality materials and they can quickly become costly. A quick fix requires less expensive materials but that's not going to provide long-term value for the community.

So the foundation and the roof are the two main points of interest. When the work is completed will it be notable for its quality or for what we call "the painted pig", which means it looks good on the outside but it has foundation and structural problems. I wouldn't just slap some paint on, put a carpet down and call it a day's work. I would want to make sure that what I'm selling to people is actually quality work so I don't bother with houses that may have structural or plumbing issues. Electrical work is something that can be updated with a good electrician, but I try to steer clear of those too because it just takes a lot more work and, again, makes it more challenging to bring value to the neighborhood.

Shannon:
I think there are some people who don't care and they can take that six months. So, why not?

Susa:
Somebody might want to do all the work themselves and they have the skills which is great. But I want to leverage my time, money and

energy. I don't know anything about being an electrician so I need to rely heavily on the professionals in that field.

Shannon:
What are some creative strategies you use when trying to acquire a property?

Susa:
Creative ways to find homes is by simply talking to people. I tell everybody I know that I am looking for a home. Somebody will have a friend, an aunt, a neighbor, a contact that is useful to me. I'll hear something through the grapevine or someone else will and call me. That's the best way to find property. It's a simple as talking to people.

Another way I find properties is by scouring sites that are similar to Craigslist where people are posting, "Hey, I'm selling my house." If it's not connected to a real estate agent, they're trying to sell by owner, which means they want to save money and that is something I can help them do.

Shannon:
Can you explain how a short sale works?

Susa:
Short sale is a process to stop a foreclosure from happening. In a short sale, which can actually take a very long time, the mortgage note is settled for less than the amount that is owed. Say we have a house that is owed $150,000 and the family is in dire need and financially cannot make their mortgage payments. The family is six months or more behind on their mortgage payments. As an investor, I can get permission from the owner to go and talk to the bank on their behalf and work with the bank to settle the debt for less than $150,000. I make no promises but when we come to an agreement, the bank is happy because they get their money and the homeowner is happy because the bank is off their back and they no longer risk foreclosure, which will damage their credit for 10 years. Helping people avoid foreclosure by negotiating with the bank on their behalf is a great way to get properties.

Shannon:

"Short sale," I think people have the misconception that that means it's a short amount of time.

Susa:

Correct. That's what I thought too!

Shannon:

Short sale means that you short the amount of money owed to the bank. Is that accurate?

Susa:

That is very accurate. Before I started investing, I had no clue that a short sale referred to money owed. I was thinking, "oh sweet, I can get a house in like two weeks." It rarely happens like that because you're working with a negotiation. Sometimes the short sale could take six months, a year, or two years. It's working with a bank and helping them understand the fastest way for them to make their money back is by agreeing that they'll take $125,000 instead of $150,000 for that property.

Shannon:

What do you see on average, the length of time a short sale takes?

Susa:

Oh, if there was an average, I'd be happy. I've seen some friends complete a short sale in three weeks or a month but they already had relationships with the bank. Again, they had their network in place so the bank knew trusted the credibility and professionalism of this investor.

The same investor may work with another person for three years. If the person is in the military, he may get to a certain point and then all of a sudden get called for active duty and sent out of the country, which stops the process. The home will not risk foreclosure while he is serving his country. When he returns, the process begins again. What we can do as investors is help that short sale.

Shannon:

What is a tax lien and how can a real estate investor benefit from it?

Susa:

Everybody has to pay property taxes. As an investor, you're looking at the different property taxes that are owed and analyzing their numbers to find the one that you can benefit from by becoming "the bank." I am going to be the one buying that tax note. Then I just basically become the bank. The money is owed to me with interest. This is a perfect way because either my money comes back to me after I bought that tax lien or the property comes to me. Either way my money is working for me.

Shannon:

If a person is behind on their taxes they can lose their home?

Susa:

Yes. They can lose their home because of taxes. Our biggest expense in life is going to be our taxes. The government doesn't want to give up any of its share. That's how we take care of the roads, build our schools, our police force and our fire department. Taxes cover our public servants so people will run into serious issues if they don't pay their taxes.

Shannon:

Do you feel that real estate investing success is dependent on a strong economy?

Susa:

No. I do not think that is the case. A strong economy just means that other people around you are feeling confident about the real estate market, but there are specific strategies to apply in a rising market, a sustained market or a declining market.

The great recession of 2008-2009 was a great time to invest in real estate. Short sales were huge because banks were saying, "I just loaned $200,000 on a house. I've gotten $25,000 back on it but now the owners haven't paid $20,000 in payments." They're looking at it going, okay that's months, years of payments on some houses and I'm not getting my money. They were eager to negotiate short sales. Then those investors were turning those houses into rentals and a cash flowing business.

Shannon:

That makes sense. Do you almost feel like investing is better in a not-so-strong economy?

Susa:

I think it's better to have the education and the knowledge to work in all types of economies. There are always people to network with, deals to find and value to add regardless of market conditions. Knowing the strategies for each of the types of markets will always allow you to be successful.

Shannon:

How has your knowledge and education in real estate changed the way you invest?

Susa:

It's changed everything about how I invest. I used to be so focused on the stocks and what my 401K was losing, and that was stressing me out. I mean, sleepless nights worried about my future. Now that I'm involved in real estate investment and working with other people in any kind of market, I have peace of mind. I get to help others and make money at the same time.

Shannon:

What type of legacy do you want to leave behind?

Susa:

One of my favorite quotes is by Marianne Williamson, "Our deepest fear is not that we are inadequate. Our deepest fear is that we are powerful beyond measure. It is our light, not our darkness, that most frightens us. We ask ourselves, who am I to be brilliant, gorgeous, talented, fabulous? Actually, who are you not to be? You are a child of God. Your playing small doesn't serve the world. There is nothing enlightened about shrinking so other people won't feel insecure around you. We are all meant to shine, as children do. We were born to make manifest the glory of God within us. It's not just in some of us; it's in everyone. And as we let our light shine, we unconsciously give others permission to do the same. As we are liberated from our own fear, our presence automatically liberates others."

I first read those words when I was 21-years-old. I was dealing with all of the typical dramas of any young woman that age. Then I read that and realized that there are so many things that people miss out on in life because they're worried about making others feel bad, so much so that they keep themselves down.

We've talked and mentioned that a lot of my life is about helping other people and networking and bringing others up. The more that people know this, the more that everybody can start making sure everybody around them is better and lifting everybody up. If I can work with people and have them understand that concept about them, then they can go help other people. It will be just like rain in a puddle, one drop in the water causes a ripple effect, and the same can happen in a pond or an entire lake. The wave just continues. More lives are touched. More lives are changed. And everybody's self-worth and self-image is elevated.

Shannon:
What advice would you give someone who is allowing fear to hold them back to start their real estate investing?

Susa:
I would say, "I know exactly how you feel." There is a game that is called Cash Flow and I like to describe it as real-life Monopoly on steroids. The first time I played it, I could not want to be out of that room faster. I was so afraid of debt. I had people telling me all the time that debt was bad and it was going to be the downfall of me and nothing good can be done with debt. In this game it is using the

liability of buying an apartment building or buying a four-plex which is like townhouses and using that to better my income.

Doing that, I could not have ran farther away from it ... I wanted to go tuck in a corner. I was so scared; it was fake money! The more I listened to the people around me and the more I played it, the more I realized that my fear of debt was holding me back. It was not benefiting me or benefiting my friends and family. It was limiting me. I put a glass ceiling over myself. I put my limitations on me. As I broke free of that fear and realized that as I faced my fear through the game and rose, which is now what I think of when I hear fear, is to face everything and rise. We can overcome it.

False evidence that appears real; that fear, that false evidence doesn't help anybody. Playing small doesn't help and it's not making me the person that I can be. As I get out of my comfort zone or what my friend Bob has said, my dead zone, great things happen outside of that fear. Feel the fear and do it anyways. Feel that fear, get out and try. Find out there's so much more that you can do.

Seth McGovern

Seth McGovern is a successful entrepreneur and real estate investor. His point of view is consistently ahead of the curve and sought after by major business and technology publications, as it has been for over 20 years. While this chapter marks his first endeavor into a printed volume; he will be finishing his first book later this year, with a second close behind. Originally from Boston, with travels around the world, he is a global citizen and one of today's remarkable thought leaders.

Contact Info:
Email: reibook@sethmcgovern.com

Shannon:

What inspired you to get into real estate?

Seth:

I have read enough to know that most successful people either made their fortunes in real estate or acquired lots of real estate to grow their fortune. That is what piqued my initial financial interest. Before that, I always loved architecture, buildings, and houses. Since I was young, I have been drawing cars, buildings, and houses. I've always been intrigued by architecture.

Shannon:

So when you were little, and your teacher asked, "What do you want to be when you grow up?" what did you say?

Seth:

I answered, "The boss." The teacher actually told my mother that was the first time she'd ever heard an answer like that. I had a reason though, and to this day, it still makes perfect sense. My mother always said that the boss got all the money and didn't have to do any work, which sounded great to me!

Shannon:

Has that come true for you?

Seth:

Yeah. I started my first company at twenty-three, so I've been the boss for a while.

Shannon:

When you started your first company, what was that?

Seth:

My first company was in technology, and actually, before that I was a boss. I managed an Information Technology department when I was nineteen. I kind of grew up in, and made my initial money with information technology.

Shannon:

Would you say that leaders are born or leaders are developed?

Seth:

I think there's a bit of both. I believe there are definitely character traits that some people have; however, they can be developed as well. With enough training, the right education, and determination, even folks who aren't natural born leaders can grow into them.

Shannon:

How has your education in real estate changed the way that you invest?

Seth:

The investments are no longer a mystery or guess; I know the numbers up front and understand I can get paid out now or have cash over time. I understand the options ahead of time.

From renting my first place at eighteen, to doing my first project when I was twenty-two, where I actually built some townhouses, I thought I knew a lot about real estate. With that project, I was going to live in one and build another one next to it for income. Then I ended up doing some condominiums. I had a number of friends in the construction industry when I was younger. Many of my friends were in the trades, and I ended up spending a lot of weekends ripping down walls, installing windows, and remodeling bathrooms. I was helping friends out, all through my twenties. In my late twenties, I started a condo project where we bought some units, rehabbed them, and turned them into time-shares with one of the top time-share companies in the world.

Shannon:

Would it be correct to say that your daily living was in IT, but your passion was in real estate?

Seth:

That would be an accurate statement, because even in my twenties, I was looking at land deals and thinking about building.

Shannon:

Would you go back in time and redo it all the same way, or would you change it based on the education you have now?

Seth:

I would definitely change it. There's a little more to this story. I actually retired when I was twenty-nine from tech. I made enough money and had a few companies that provided residual income. I didn't have to work because of that success, so I didn't. If I were at that point, knowing what I know now, I would have invested a lot more money in real estate. I would have been taking my residuals and buying and building houses and having them develop more cash. I would also be taking investment monies and redirecting them into real estate deals. I never play the whole, "Oh, I want to go back," or have regrets game. I'm not that type of person; however, to answer your question, yes, I'd do it differently with the knowledge that I have now.

Shannon:

What kind of acquisition strategies are you using right now?

Seth:

I'm starting new developments, so land acquisitions primarily. Currently, I'm looking at a Veterans' Project with a number of partners in Colorado. I'm also doing fix-and-flips and multi-units in Boston and Chicago.

The Veterans' Project is a turn-key, build to suit, senior veterans' community which will have close to 200 units when it's complete.

Shannon:

Do you think that with that Veterans' Project you will do more renting, or do you think you'll do lease to own lease options?

Seth:

The rental model would provide cash, long-term, over time. The lease option allows the tenant the same type of payments, but they are paying a lease and they have the option of taking over the property. This can be either a balloon payment or a paid out over time with financing. We are still working out the numbers, with a few different scenarios.

Shannon:

Why would somebody do a lease option with you versus just standard financing?

Seth:

The purchaser has more options. They're leasing up front and essentially trying out the property, while having part of their monthly payment go toward the option to buy the property. They could also work out flexible terms with the owner, along with avoiding traditional bank financing and its stringent approval process; which is good for self-employed or other non-traditional income earners.

Shannon:

What advice would you give to someone who wanted to get into multi-family dwellings?

Seth:

That's where this education would have been amazing twenty years ago. There were many things back then that would have been good to know. For instance, costing out the project, getting background on the builder and projects that they have done before, and many things that really go into getting the numbers right. If there's any information that anyone can get at any time about calculating deals and insuring that there's good value in a project, that's always beneficial. Especially early on, so you can make informed decisions.

Shannon:

If I came to you and I said, "Hey, I've just found this great little house. They're asking $150,000 but it needs about $20,000 worth of work. I could probably get it for $100,000 and put $20,000 into it, I've got $30,000 profit, right?"

Seth:

Not necessarily. Where are those numbers coming from? Do you have comps for the area? What's the $20,000 worth of work? Is that a kitchen and a bathroom? Is that putting on a deck? Is that re-doing a basement? All of those things can run into additional costs. Decks usually aren't as risky, but you get into bathrooms and kitchens, and you find you need to bring electrical up to code, or you need to bring plumbing up to code. That's not just for the project area that you're working on, it's for the rest of the house. You start touching electrical or plumbing, and next thing you know, the town could potentially want you to upgrade the electrical or the plumbing for the rest of the house.

Your financing could be another piece. If you're bank financing the real estate and talking about owning this property, you're going to pay the amount that you're putting in a loan, over again. For example, if you're talking about financing $100,000, at the end of the day when you do a standard bank loan, you're going to be paying about $200,000 back. That amount just increases with the amount you borrow. $300,000 turns into $600,000, etc. Those are big numbers that people rarely look at. Most people with a mortgage never really understand how much they actually pay for their mortgage overall.

Shannon:
Why would a real estate investor invest in tax liens?

Seth:
You can control a property for a small sum of money; If you manage that tax debt, you can then gain control of the property. Since you have taken over the lien, you can do all kinds of great stuff from there. You can rehab them, or if there is someone living there, you can work out financing with them to keep them in their place; there are lots of options, which is always nice. You know, with any deal, but especially in real estate, it's nice to have options because you don't always in other areas. If you buy an older property, you pretty much have to fix and flip it, the rehab kind of angle, or try to just make a little profit by flipping it to somebody else who's going to fix and flip, or rehab. Typically, the options are pretty clear and somewhat limited in a lot of deals right from the beginning, but with tax liens, you have more options around the different things you can do with the property

since the acquisition cost is so low. Alternatively, if the tax is paid, you receive your lien amount back, plus a fixed interest rate.

Shannon:

So if you buy a person's tax lien, because they're behind on their property taxes but they're not behind on their house payment you own that home?

Seth:

Yes, if you buy the tax lien, you'll either get interest when they pay it back or you can own that house for the amount you bought the lien for. Factors around interest and timing vary by state, so it's always good to check local laws first.

Shannon:

What do you think is the number one reason that people fail at real estate?

Seth:

The number one reason people fail is lack of knowledge. People don't understand the various aspects of real estate and therefore don't get that it's a long-term position. When people first get started, they are excited! Excitement is great, but excitement only lasts for a month, maybe two, or possibly four if they're really enthusiastic. I've rarely seen excitement last more than that. At some point, even the most excited, enthusiastic, and tenacious people have difficulty keeping excitement up when it's not working. If they had an expectation, that it was going to be easy and they were going to make a million dollars in two months, it's just unrealistic. It's not about getting rich quick; it's about getting rich the right way.

Using methodical, clear choices, based on good background information, solid knowledge, and accurate numbers is a recipe for success. Part of the excitement comes from TV. Reality TV, however, is not reality. I have never been able to buy a house for $20,000, put $20,000, into it, and then turn around and sell it for $150,000. They never show the ones on TV that they spend 80 on, then 30 to fix, and then have a hard time selling for 100. There are a number of those, which is why you need to know your numbers along with being excited.

Shannon:
As a real estate investor, do you like those TV shows, or do you feel like they are misleading?

Seth:
I think most of TV is misleading, but it's entertainment. It's not edutainment. There are very few channels that are actually out to educate people or provide knowledge. They are mostly providing entertainment. Overall, I like them to a certain degree, because they make me more money and increase interest in real estate.

Shannon:
What type of legacy do you want to leave?

Seth:
For me there are a couple of aspects to legacy. There's the easy part, which is financial, which is what most people go to, and having options for my children and my children's children, so that they don't have to struggle in life. The other side of it, however, is a lot more meaningful. For me it is more around what legacy really looks like. I don't have to have my name on buildings, for example; however, I would like to leave some properties. I want to leave a legacy of property for people to have a place to live, and financially, for people to do it in a sound way; so that they're not in another bubble with all kind of false rates and dishonest mortgage brokers and companies, telling them they could afford a bunch more than they could. I think the legacy of the properties that I house people in and my partners house people in are sound investments, which make sense for them and don't put us into another bubble that isn't sustainable.

Overall, I want to be known as honorable, caring, and straight.

That's a real legacy.

Michael Myer

Michael Myer has many years in Real Estate investing, stock market investing, budgeting, and financial stewardship. He resides in North Carolina running his multiple businesses and building his real estate portfolio. Most of his portfolio is directed towards commercial buy and holds, with the intention to increase his residential buy and holds.

Mr. Myer is a Marine Reservist with the MOS 6114 Light Attack Helicopter Mechanic. He drills out of Joint Base McGuire-Dix-Lakehurst in New Jersey with HMLA-773 Det Minus. The helicopters he works on are the AH1-W Cobra and the UH1-Y Huey. He is also avid in the fitness community as a certified CrossFit instructor and USAW Sports Performance coach.

He enjoys adventures, spending time with his loved ones, and traveling to new countries and immersing himself in different cultures.

Contact info:
Email: mrmyer@equalitycap.co

Shannon:
What inspired you to get into real estate investing?

Michael:
My parents did some real estate investing before I was born and they always thought it was a great market, however, they were generally investing as a hobby. They were never really invested as a career. I just started trying to learn more about it. I heard about Donald Trump and Robert Kiyosaki and what they were doing. Their theories of investing for cash flow and the potential that passive income will create for you are the things that really piqued my interest.

My parents and I did one fix and flip together. We inherited a house from one of my father's family friends and we fixed it, flipped it all by ourselves. She was a smoker, so we had to gut the whole house. It took us no more than a couple of weeks to renovate. We then were able to sell it quickly and make a good profit. That definitely solidified the fact that I wanted to invest in real estate as a career. Once I was able to see the income, it really got me going.

Shannon:
When you learned of the opportunity to fix and flip your first home, did you just go down to your local library, make a list, and figure out what to do?

Michael:
No, that was a long time ago. My dad has so much experience with building, engineering, contracting, and working with his hands. We were able to do most of the improvements ourselves. The only thing that we didn't do was the installation of the flooring. We may not have done things perfectly from a numbers perspective. We kind of just got it, put it together and then sold it. We didn't do any sort of education or analytics prior to beginning.

Shannon:
How do you think your education in real estate has changed the way that you invest?

Michael:

My education has mostly changed the way that I analyze deals and my purchasing strategies. I have learned to pay a lot more attention to running the numbers and having multiple exit strategies before a purchase is even made. I don't ever want to end up being stuck paying multiple mortgages on properties that aren't producing any income. My education taught me to focus more attention on the numbers and acquisition strategies.

Shannon:

What advice would you give someone who wants to get started in real estate investing but has little or no money or bad credit?

Michael:

The first thing that they have to do is actually get an education. In this case, specifically for financing. Having an education allows you to put together deals without having a lot of access to funds. It helps you build a team of investors and other knowledgeable individuals that you could bounce ideas off of. It gives you the access to the strategies that you could use, such as owner financing.

They should also find a mentor and become part of real estate investing communities. A common phrase is "Your network equals your net worth." It is absolutely crucial to have a good team around you before jumping in. I also recommend a great real estate attorney skilled in the multi-faceted realm of creative acquisitions, as well as a knowledgeable tax strategist and CPA.

Shannon:

Tell me a little bit more about owner financing. Why would a homeowner want to finance the sale of their own home?

Michael:

There are a couple of reasons why a seller will finance their own home. For example, if they are having a difficult time selling it, if they have a low interest rate and they end up charging the buyer a higher interest rate, they may have a prepayment penalty or a tax issue if they sell their home early. There are multiple reasons. When a seller finances the home for you in essence, the seller becomes the bank. You have to work out an interest rate and a payment schedule for when the home will be completely paid for. If you are able to get a seller to finance the home and you are going to rent out the property it is crucial to make sure your numbers add up. This is a great strategy because your tenant is paying down your mortgage for you while the home is also appreciating in value. However, just because you can get owner financing doesn't mean that it's the right deal.

Shannon:
What are some other creative ways to acquire a property?

Michael:
There are other creative ways to find properties such as pre-fore-closures, foreclosures, going down to the courthouse, tax auctions, and networking. You can also use a wholesaler. Wholesalers can find great deals! They either don't have the experience or don't want to fix and flip, so they'll just quickly off-load a house. They get to make some money on their side and you still have the opportunity to make good money as well.

Shannon:
You live in North Carolina. Do you only invest locally?

Michael:
At the moment, yes. I am focused mostly on commercial properties right now. Eventually, I would like to add some residential properties to my portfolio. I have great property right now that is a commercial warehouse which I rent to a manufacturing firm.

There's more money in commercial investing, but there's a little bit more security in residential simply because people will always need a place to live. It is more common to see commercial properties that are waiting to be leased rather than residential units that are waiting to be rented. Generally, the time span is a lot longer between tenants in a commercial rental than tenants in a residential rental.

Since there is more downtime the rental cost is higher but there's more opportunity to make money on the commercial side. It is also very important to have a good location.

Another great strategy is to combine the two, commercial and residential, by investing in multi-unit properties, such as apartment complexes and hotel/resorts. When you have a multi-unit property, you have 1 property that has, let's say, 4 doors and each door is making $1,000. That property is pulling $4,000 per month when fully occupied. It is very rare that you can find one single family home that pulls in the same amount as a multi-unit for the same total footprint.

With multi-unit dwellings you can also utilize height. You're using the same land footprint but you can build higher. Just think of how much that can change the potential of the property! There's a lot more opportunity to make money there.

If you have 1 acre of land and you can build a building that's 10 stories, 50 stories, 100 stories and so on, you can obviously fit a lot more people in multi-stories than you would be able to with just 1 floor on that same plot of land. When you can do more with less land, that's the best way to go. You can always build higher. You cannot create land but you can create space.

Shannon:

Do you feel like real estate investing success depends on a strong economy?

Michael:

Success in real estate does not depend on a strong economy, no. However, the strength or status of the economy is going to dictate which strategies you're using for your investing. That's why it's so important to have multiple strategies at your disposal to create wealth in real estate.

When the economy is strong, people are going to have more opportunity to buy property, so you have more opportunity to sell property (e.g.; wholesaling; fix and flip; lease option). In a weaker economy, people are generally going to have to rent because they're not going to have the capital or the banks will not be lending as freely as they would in a strong economy. You're going to have a bigger rental market.

When you're investing in a fix and flip, that makes your exit strategy a sale. But if you're holding it for, say, 8 months, proper-ties aren't moving and the market in that area is going down. It's over-saturated. Nobody is buying, everybody is trying to sell. Then, at that point, you can switch to a buy and hold strategy and you can just use it as a rental property or a buy and hold.

Ultimately, you still do want to off-load that property from your portfolio. So now you can adjust that strategy to a lease option. This is where the people who are the tenants of the property become the potential buyers. You can discuss it with them if they're interested in purchasing the home. They can purchase the option to buy the house. You can even credit some of the rental income towards the purchase.

If you don't have the initial sale strategy, you can always do the buy and hold strategy. If you have private money lenders, they may not like the buy and hold, though. Always communicate with your investors if that's your current funding.

Shannon:
Would you say that someone should put together a lease option on their own or they should have a team of people that help them?

Michael:
I don't think investors should do anything alone, really. Investors (even hobbyists, probably more so) should have a team that they can master-mind with and bounce ideas off. Unless you're the person in the group who is the expert in lease options, then no, I wouldn't recommend doing it alone. I think everyone should always have a lot of help putting every-thing together to make sure everything is in your best interests.

If you are an expert, then you should have people helping you with more remedial tasks. Teamwork makes the dream work.

Shannon:
It sounds to me like you have a team that you probably mastermind with.

Michael:
Yes.

I have been part of mastermind groups for a couple of years now. They are always uplifting and educational. You are able to master needed leadership skills to be a true professional. One of the best masterminds that I have attended was about self-promotion and branding.

Shannon:

It sounds like leadership is really important to you. What do you think makes a strong leader in real estate?

Michael:

There are keys to leadership that transfer to all industries. Knowledge, initiative, fairness, stability and performing well under pressure are some of the most important leadership traits. Communication is also extremely important. A leader needs to be able to effectively and efficiently convey a message to their team while simultaneously motivating them.

Shannon:

How important do you think it is for a leader to motivate?

Michael:

I think it is very important for a leader to motivate. I also feel that self-motivation is equally important. If you don't have the motivation to get out there and seek something better for yourself, no one will do it for you. You're just allowing the opportunities to pass you by.

That's a choice that you have. If you choose to be unmotivated, that's fine. People can do whatever they want, but the lack of action is a choice. That goes to the action consequence matrix. There is a consequence of action, there is also a consequence of inaction.

Shannon:

Define the word "success" for me.

Michael:

Success in my world would have to be living comfortably, stress-free and having the financial independence as well as time/location independence. I don't have to have $100,000,000.00 in the bank, but as long as my bills are being paid, my cash flow is paying for my life-style and you still have some pocket money to travel and spend time with friends and family. That would have to be the ultimate definition of success for me.

Shannon:
What motivates you every day?

Michael:
That definition of success and being able to provide for my family and friends. I want to be a good role model and leave a good legacy for my family. I want to teach them the proper way to be in charge of their finances and not having to have a common W2 job. They can do it being an entrepreneur and that's the best way.

Shannon:
What's the best piece of advice that you have ever been given?

Michael:
To understand what drives you emotionally and focus on satisfying those needs. Then things will fall into place after that. If you're constantly happy, you're in a better state to make decisions. As long as you're supporting the things that keep you happy, then you'll be making the best decisions for yourself and for the people around you.

Also, who wants to go into business with people that are constantly unhappy? Misery loves company and those people will flood negative energy into you. You must repel the negativity at all costs. Stay positive. Be happy.

Shannon:
What is the best piece of advice your dad has ever given you?

Michael:
Wow, that is a difficult question. He has given me so much great advice. The best piece of advice is you just have to get out and do it on your own. Stop asking if you're "allowed to" do this or, "Do you

think we can do it?" and just make a decision. Take ownership. Do it. Then show them that it was the right thing by the success that it creates. Basically, be in charge of your own reality. Do not ask for permissions to create.

Shannon:

When you think about your life, when you think about the legacy that you are building, what legacy do you want to leave behind?

Michael:

I want to be remembered as somebody who was willing to do whatever it took to better the lives of the team or the family or the friendships around. Making the hard decisions that others don't necessarily want to make. Being held accountable if one of those decisions was the wrong decision.

I want to be remembered as an individual with integrity, honor, and courage. I'm going to borrow from my Marine Corps experience here. We have very strict standards. We are the guardians of the standards of excellence. I want to be remembered as someone with whom upheld my end of that.

Celest Secrist

Armed with a BS in Business Management from San Diego State University and a MBA in Executive Leadership from Ellis University, Celest Secrist analyzed 100 property deals in 2015 alone. In the process, the relationships she has built in the industry has complimented her business partners in different real estate ventures which focus on vacation rental assets for passive income and residential rehabbing to help corporate professional earn a great ROI on their liquid and/or retirement funds. All her real estate venture partnerships are run thru their Living a Blessed Life, Inc. company.

Family and strong relationships form the foundation for Celest Secrist's approach to life. She's been married for 10 years to her husband Jonathan Secrist. She also has 3 beautiful children. Running a successful business from home, Celest also makes time to assist with her church's Mommy-N-Me Women's Bible Study small group and actively participate alongside her children in canned food, school supply, Operation Christmas Child mission activities to teach them to take care of other families/children in need.

Contact Info:
Email: celest@livingablessedlifeinc.com
Web: www.livingablessedlifeinc.com

What inspired you to get into real estate investing?

Celest:
Ever since I was little girl, my mom always said, "Oh you have the Cometa business blood in you. Out of all your sisters, you have that business side more than them." That's my mother's side of the family who have thrived on business ventures throughout the family's history. I remember my first crack at a business was making drawer potpourri sachets for the 5-star resort my mother worked for when I was in high school. Boy, was that an experience! My hands smelled like potpourri for weeks after each shipment!

Real Estate, in general, popped on my radar when I was exploring options for my entrepreneur class paper that required me to do a SWOT analysis on a potential business I wanted to pursue. That's when I met a mortgage broker while working at the credit union. We got to talking about what he does and my class, which eventually led to him agreeing to do an interview with me for my paper. I've got to say that during that interview, I was so intrigued by everything he did to help people get into their first home or help them secure their new home in a new place for the next part of their lives, whether as a couple, family, or independent business professional. And I worked at a financial institution, so, of course, I oddly love working with numbers. Even after I did all that work on that paper, I was so content with where I was in life, nothing really pushed me to pursue my dream. I was enjoying a progressing career in the banking industry, I got married, I finished my bachelor's and master's degrees. But what turned me back to real estate and investing in particular was the birth of my 3 beautiful children with my husband, Jonathan. I want to be completely honest: we were not ready financially to have children.

We even struggled for a few years making ends meet. Trying to find ways to contribute to our family's income, I finally realized that the traditional corporate job was not feasible for us due to the cost of daycare for 3 infants. Interestingly enough, I was talking with my mother again, and she asked if there was anything I could do from home. That's when I started thinking of starting a business once again, and real estate was the first on the list. I was so set on getting my real estate license to the point where I was even enrolled in the next class through the community college. Then I started thinking about real estate investing because that's what my mother's side of the family does in the Philippines, but in commercial property. I eventually came across an opportunity to learn from multiple real estate investor mentors, which opened my eyes to the exact solution to our financial hardship.

So I made the decision to learn real estate investing from the best of the best in the business who would be willing to mentor me and teach me their systems. That's how I got started. And I am truly grateful for the expertise and knowledge I've received, not just in one aspect of real estate investing, but all aspects which rocket-launched our business.

Shannon:
Do you think that real estate investing success is dependent on a strong economy?

Celest:
If you asked me 2 years ago, I would have said "yes," but with how much I've learned from other successful real estate investors and mentors about business financial literacy and investing, I truly believe that if you know the right strategies and you have the right tools, anyone can succeed in real estate investing in any market condition. Going back to my exploration into the real estate mortgage broker arena, I would have been a mortgage originator whose life blood of income would have been very dependent on a strong economy. When the economy tanked, I would have been out of the job like thousands of others.

Shannon:
After you acquired your first home, what was the exit strategy you used?

Celest:
The majority of our projects start as "fix and flips." "Fix and flips" create somewhat short term income or massive income. Although

they are great money, they do not create income without a lot of daily work. Interestingly enough, our "fix and flip" operations have led to other real estate strategies such as wholesaling, vacation rentals, and lending opportunities on our team's projects.

Shannon:

What is one of the tools you can use in a strong economy to make money in real estate?

Celest:

We're really excited about a new strategy, which is vacation rental operations. We're establishing a systematic process for vacation rental properties. Some of our recent projects have been located in great tourist areas such as Big Bear, CA, where we can capitalize on higher passive income potential. This strategy works in a strong economy because people are spending. They are comfortable with taking vacations because they have a little slush fund to spend.

This strategy puts us one step closer to our long term goals of obtaining a high level of passive income, which is more rewarding in the long run. It doesn't hurt that when we do take trips out to the properties, we are strongly encouraged to capitalize on business write-off benefits taught to us by our CPA & real estate attorney Mark Kohler. The biggest benefit that hits us closest to our heart is the fact that we'll have the capacity to create great family memories when we spend time at the properties ourselves. Jonathan's and my children are still quite young. They may or may not remember the little adventures we have taken them on, but as they get older, we want to create a strong family bond. As I mentioned before, we realized very quickly we were not ready financially to have children. Things were tight financially, but it was also tight on quality family time. My husband works hard 5-6 days a week, which leaves him exhausted and strapped on time between the things needed fixing around the house and spending time with the children. This strategy is allowing us to shift faster to a more passive income which will free both myself and Jonathan from certain obligations to the more important role of being present and active parents continually shaping our boys into Godly men and our girl into a Godly woman.

Shannon:
Why do "fix and flips" interest you?

Celest:
I think it's interesting how the majority of people looking to get into real estate investing are drawn to doing a "fix and flip" project. It doesn't surprise me because you see that strategy constantly promoted on mainstream channels such as HGTV. We personally love the benefits of fixing and flipping, but not just the monetary perspective. In the words of one of my mentors, "we love creating win-win-win-win-win situations." Our operation benefits so many people throughout the process.

The majority of our deals are done with private money investor's liquid or retirement funds. We help hard working corporate professionals earn higher and more secure rates of return on their assets than they would in the stock market. Our investors see on average an annualized return of investment between 15%–20%, which is a lot more than the 3%–10% they would see in the stock market plus their investment is secured by the property and the insurance we hold on the property. An added benefit to us is we do the majority of our deals with no money out of our own pockets. I believe that this is a major win-win scenario.

Once our private investor's funds are in place, we use those funds to purchase properties in need of repairs. Most properties that need fixing have a homeowner in distress. They either don't have the money to make the repairs in order to sell the property, they're unable to fulfill their mortgage obligation due to an unexpected life event, or any of the several other reasons. We help them by lifting that burden off their shoulders by agreeing on a purchase price that works for both parties. That's another win-win situation.

When it comes to rehabbing the property, who benefits? The economy. Our material costs stimulate the goods market because we need specific goods to remodel a property. Then small construction businesses benefit. We generate work and jobs for those skilled in drywall, painting, pool remodeling and maintenance, and so on. Our latest project created 6 weeks' worth of work, and we hired 8 different companies to complete specific parts of the project. This helps those individuals provide for their families' basic needs. Plus, we don't have to do the actual labor. We just need to manage the progress. I would say that's a win-win-win situation.

After all is said and done, there are a few others who benefit. Those people are the surrounding community/neighborhood, the future homeowners, and of course, our families. We help raise the home value in the neighborhood, and they don't have to deal with squatters making a neighborhood eyesore even worse. The future homeowners will have a move in ready property they can call home and not have to worry about needing to do major repairs. Finally, our families benefit because the profits we collect contributes to us having the ability to purchase everyday essentials and reaching our pre-set wealth creation goals.

Shannon:
Does your husband do the real estate investing with you?

Celest:
Jonathan has extensive knowledge in home construction, repair, and building code, so I always talk with him about what's happening on all our projects to get his feedback and guidance. This guidance is priceless, and I value him enormously.

Shannon:
Do you have a favorite "fix and flip" that you've done?

Celest:
Yes, there was a property in San Marcos that my sister and her husband purchased as their first home when they lived in San Diego. It was then rented out to family, and they built their new home and settled in Edmond, Oklahoma. Keeping the townhouse was more of a financial headache than benefit from such a long distance that they decided to sell it.

Since Jonathan and I were just starting to get our feet wet in real estate investing, we used the property to get some experience in all the processes used in real estate.

This is process we went through:

1) Finding the property
2) Analyzing the property
3) Presenting options
4) Repairing the property
5) Selling the property

Obviously, we found the property lead through family. We talked with the homeowner (sister and her husband) and gathered information on why they were selling and what they were trying to achieve. Which in this case was complete removal of the property from their care, and they wanted the mortgage off their credit. We analyzed the property using the tools our mentors recommended to estimate repairs, after repair value, fair market value, cost to hold, and cost to sell. Then we drew up 2-3 different offers using different acquisition strategies such as subject-to, purchase at a major discount, and equity sharing. All these steps we took helped set up a system to deal with other homeowners and real estate professionals. It was a great "practice" property!

The repairs were basic. Painting, deep cleaning, light landscaping maintenance, and new carpet in 2 of the 3 bedrooms. When everything was complete, they hired a Realtor to sell the property, and that agent coordinated professional pictures, an open house, and managed the paperwork for selling of the property. They were able to accept an offer within 8 days of listing the property. There were some litigation issues between the HOA and the builder, which delayed the sale. This was also a reminder to always build in money for unforeseen costs. It finally sold 6 months later.

We learned a lot of valuable lessons just by doing a dry test run. Obviously, the major one was that litigation can hold up a sale because lenders will not lend unless the problem is resolved. In the end, we got a system setup to pursue other deals that we came across.

Shannon:
If someone wanted to get started in real estate investing, and they had no money to invest, could they?

Celest:

Oh, yes! Subject-to is a creative property acquisition strategy. If I was doing a subject-to purchase, I would draw up a purchase contract that created a condition. That condition is that the current mortgage is required to stay in place. So I'm purchasing the property from the seller based on the existing mortgage, but the title of the property would change ownership to our business name.

Shannon:

Is a subject-to a wise investment strategy if you didn't know the person?

Celest:

Yes. It may take a little more to educate sellers, so they're comfortable in accepting your offer. The majority of the population has never heard of the concept, and it's not taught in our current standard school curriculum.

There are really many different ways someone can creatively acquire a property. Because every homeowner has different reasons for selling their property, the key is to find out their reason and provide a solution. Maybe they can't make their payments due a spouse passing away, divorce, or loss of a job. Maybe they don't have the funds to rehab the property to get it to a selling price that will have them walking away with a little bit of money. Maybe they are upside down on the property. Whatever the situation, I can present a solution that can help the homeowner. It's doesn't matter whether you know them or not. It's actually reliant on if you can be creative enough to come up with a viable solution. Just be aware that you may have a solution, but they may not be ready to accept it.

Shannon:

Do you ever worry that there will be a time when the bank or the mortgage company may not like that somebody else is making their payment?

Celest:

I know for a fact that there is a clause in the mortgage contract that states if you change the title out of the current homeowner name, then they can call the mortgage loan balance due in full immediately. From the bank's perspective and my work history in the industry, they very rarely, if ever, make the decision to call a loan due if the mortgage is current and being paid on time. Really, they don't care who's making the payment. Say the bank did notice the discrepancy, what course of action do they have? They call the loan due and say the loan balance isn't paid. Then the bank's recourse would be to foreclose on the property, which would incur more expenses and fees, and they may or may not get those back when they finally get the property off their books. It's a lot more headache than just letting the loan get paid on time every month.

Shannon:
What if that did happen? How would you be able to save that investment?

Celest:
Well, as any knowledgeable investor would have done, they would have run through the scenario before presenting the offer to the homeowner to see if the investment was still a viable option with other lending, private funds, etc. So all you would be doing is shifting to Plan B. This is where having a team and community of investors around you can come in handy because you've built relationships with individuals that may have private funds, or is a mortgage broker, or is a hard money broker, or create a partnership with an individual who has an excellent credit score and is willing let you utilize it for a reasonable return. Those are all options. But if you are financially literate in your business, you would also have resources built up that you can tap into such as business credit lines, self-directed Health Savings Accounts, or self-directed 401K/IRA/Roth accounts.

Shannon:
Other than a subject-to, what are some creative ways to acquire a property?

Celest:
I have to say, when I first started learning the fundamentals for real estate investing and business, I was blown away with how many

creative ways there were to owning or controlling real estate properties. And how you use the individual strategies or combination of strategies is all based on asking specific questions and creating a solution for an owner's problem. There is Equity Sharing, which we use in our rehab projects, so the majority of our deals are done with no money out of our own pockets. And another strategy that has caught my eye is the master lease strategy where you can control the property's cash flow, but not necessarily the property ownership.

Those are just a few of the ways you can own or control properties. Again, just focus on how you can help the homeowner and have it still benefit you.

Shannon:
How do you find these people? Is it just a needle in a haystack?

Celest:
Really, it's about getting the word out there that you're a real estate investor, and you're able to pay cash for properties. You've got to be willing to talk about it. People think that they don't know a lot of people, but when you think about your sphere of influence that can range from the bagger at the grocery store to coworkers you knew from prior jobs you possessed... it starts to add up. One of my mentors always says, "Talk to anyone and everyone and just hand them a business card. Eventually, you'll come cross someone in need of your help. Or they'll give your card to someone they know that could use your help."

Our current project properties have come from relationships we've built within the real estate industry, whether it's a private money broker, a service vendor we constantly use, or an REO acquisition firm. These people have already dealt with the bank or homeowner, and the property is ready to be assigned to a rehabber.

Shannon:
When you were first getting started, you didn't necessarily have all of those relationships in place? Did you do any sort of marketing to get it out there that you were available?

Celest:

Honestly, I didn't do any marketing. When we were getting started, my husband and I knew we could bring a lot of value to the table with his construction background and my lending and business background. We were missing that experience piece, so we joined a local community of real estate professionals eager to work with each other to be successful and that's when we met our current business partner, Jenny Brandt. She has many connections in the real estate industry because she has been rehabbing properties for over 30 years. We were looking for someone with a strong foundation, so we slowly built a relationship to the point where we both saw the benefits/value the other partner can bring. Eventually over time, her connections became our connections.

Shannon:

Let's switch gears for a second. Are a master lease and a lease option the same thing?

Celest:

No, they're not. The master lease strategy is not about holding title to the property, but more about you renting the property from the owner and subletting the space. For example, the townhouse in San Marcos where my sister and brother-in-law are out of state. I could have negotiated a master lease for 2 years where I would satisfy their monthly mortgage payment of $1800 each month during that term, hypothetically. I don't necessarily want to live there because we have our own house, but I know from my research, rent in the area is running about $2800 per month. So I find a renter and sublet the space to the new renter from $2800 per month. Each month, I'll collect the $2800, pay $1800 to my sister and her husband, and I'll positively cash flow $1000 per month without owning the property at all for 2 years. At no point did I ever hold title, but I did benefit from the arrangement a total of $24,000 over the 2-year period. This strategy works even better with multi-family units.

Now, the lease option strategy is 2 different contracts. One contract is to lease the property from the owner for, let's say, a period of 2 years. At the end of that term, you have an option contract to purchase the property from the owner for a set price of $375,000. In the same example of the townhouse in San Marcos, I could do the exact same thing during the 2-year lease period and rent it out for $2800 per month. But at the end of the 2 years, the value of the property went up to $400,000. If I exercise my option to purchase for the price of $375,000 and I have a buyer wanting to pay $399,000 for the place, I can make $24,000 from the rents and an additional $24,000 due to the appreciation on the property.

Shannon:

What is your short-term goal for your real estate investing and what is your long-term goal?

Celest:

Short-term goals… when we first got married and had our kids, we went from a dual income household to a one income household with my husband running his handyman business. The income was not very steady at all, so we ended up actually filing bankruptcy.

Because of that, obviously, our credit is not where it should be. So our short-term goals right now would be repairing that credit to the point where we're able to qualify for lending products at the best rates. Actually, taking the tools we've learned from our credit management mentor through the education that we have and implementing those strategies/steps to get our credit where it should be, like I said, to qualify for mortgages or other lending products that we can leverage wisely to accelerate our business more.

In the meantime, we're currently working on another part of our short-term goals, which is building our business credit. Business credit is another resource capable of commanding larger lending amounts because they play by very different rules than you would have on the personal credit side. By building those financial avenues, we are able to sustain our business for years to come. That's short term.

Long-term goals for our investing business is in the next 3 to 5 years is doing 15-20 rehabs a year for short term income generation. Also picking up at least 2 rental properties a year in order to build our personal portfolio of passive income for long term wealth creation, income replacement, and build an inheritance to pass on to our children and our children's children. Looking further down the road to about 7-10 years from now, we would like to shift to multi-family instead of single family investments and other business investments not limited to just real estate.

Shannon:
What type of legacy do you want to leave?

Celest:
That I was able to help others in a positive and practical way and that I truly cared about their situation. I want to be an inspiration to my children. That they can do exactly what they feel is their passion and what they believe their role is in this life and in this world. Their dream doesn't have to be hindered by how much they make or their financial situation. If they want to do missions trips overseas because that's what they love then they can do that because their parents instilled in them on the Godly character, knowledge, and wisdom they need to greatly impact this world for the better.

What I really want is for them to say that I inspired and supported them to be great. That my husband and I learned from our trails to build a stronger foundation for them to stand on and to be able to provide for themselves and their families while living their dreams.

Michelle Stiff

Michelle Stiff is a real estate investor, public school teacher, a mother, and a wife. Although she wears many hats, her passion is real estate investing. She and her husband, Jesse, first dabbled in the market in 1998, purchasing two flats for passive income, then a single family home, all in one year. Michelle Stiff is a mentor and local business woman, offering various services in real estate, from investing to property management. Michelle firmly believes in empowering people to overcome reservations as first time investors and to learn how to build their own financial independence. Being a real estate investor herself, she has the determination and drive to empower and educate other investors which makes her a valuable asset to the real estate investment team that she's a member of.

Michelle and her team work with investors on all facets of real estate from single family properties, tax liens, deeds, wholesale, investing with investors on fix and flip deals, and multi-units. No matter the level of experience, the mandate is to ensure every real estate investor secures the right team when becoming a geographical specialist and building their portfolio.

Michelle has been married to husband Jesse for 19 years and is the mother of three sons, Ameen, Leon, and Bill.

Shannon:

What inspired you to get into real estate investing?

Michelle:

Real Estate allows you to create wealth in any economy. Today's investing profit allows you to create a dependable and growing flow of income. When choosing an investment, you must weigh the amounts of income such as rents, dividends or interest that the investment is likely to yield relative to other potential investments. For example, is the tenant that I put into my home going to be able to afford the rent? I need to make sure that I set them up for success. Will it grow over time? Will it protect you against inflation? I know that if I research carefully, I can invest in any property and it will provide a profit-generating future.

Shannon:

How has your education in real estate changed the way that you invest?

Michelle:

The majority of real estate deals involve negotiated transactions. Each buyer and seller must confront his or her own personal needs, pressure, time schedule, financial worries, capabilities, interests, knowledge, and objectives. Real estate education has taught me that every property presents unique physical features, locations, and potential for improvement. More importantly, my education has given me the confidence that I needed to start investing. When I have the tools that I need to confidently use "comp" prices as a guide it is a lot easier than trying to guess if I have good information. As a result, we as investors who buy with the best information, knowledge, perseverance and imagination, do earn superior returns. The key is to shop carefully, and to systematically compare properties, seek out motivated or uninformed sellers and negotiate skillfully, and with that, you will put together great deals that include a bargain price, bargain financing, or maybe both.

Shannon:

What is one of the top real estate strategies that you have learned?

Michelle:

The top real estate strategy I've learned is called a subject-to strategy. With a subject-to strategy, the homeowner assigns ownership rights to a buyer but the seller keeps the note in his/her name. The buyer assumes ownership and makes payments on the mortgage on behalf of the seller. Since I have a great network I get to consult with great RE attorneys to make sure that I am following all of the latest RE laws. A subject-to transaction also offers an alternative to traditional financing and allows the seller to get out from under their mortgage note.

Shannon:

How has real estate changed your life?

Michelle:

It has given me a feeling of security for my retirement. No one knows the future for retirement plans, social security, stocks, bond returns, and inflation. As long the population and the economy increases, rental housing will provide the safest and surest path to both short and long term real estate wealth and a dependable return on investment. I know that I can control my real estate investments to create positive cash flow, and with that I can retire comfortably.

Shannon:

What are some creative ways to acquire a property?

Michelle:

There are copious real estate strategies, but honestly, there are some I favor more than others. I enjoy the control that the lease option acquisition strategy gives me. The ability for the property and sublease to cover payments, sell your option, or simultaneous closing. The other strategy that I love is wholesaling; You find the deal, put it under contract, and sell the contract to a cash buyer. Quick, potentially easy money. I say potentially because if you have all of your investors lined up and you have your properties "pre-sold," it is easy.

Shannon:

If you are starting with little money or poor credit what are some strategies to get into real estate?

Michelle:

Buying real estate definitely costs money, but it doesn't have to be your own money. With the right mix of resourcefulness, creativity and knowledge, you can buy real estate with poor credit and none of your own money. For example: a lease option is a strategy used in real estate to buy homes from motivated sellers without actually taking legal ownership. Instead, the real estate investor signs a long term lease with the homeowner as well as signing a legal option to buy the property at a locked-in price in the future. The investor can easily rent the property out which creates a cash flow. If they don't want to do that they can find a buyer to sell to.

Shannon:

What is the number one mistake an individual makes when buying their first investment property?

Michelle:

The number one mistake is definitely a lack of research. Before most individuals buy a car or television, they compare different models and ask questions to determine whether or not what they are about to purchase is indeed worth the money. The due diligence that goes into purchasing an investment property should be more rigorous.

Shannon:

When you began your real estate investing career how important was it to establish a team to help you be successful?

Michelle:

Real estate investment is not a solitary investment. I could not be successful without a whole team of professionals. Knowing who you need on the team and the role, they should fulfill is of the utmost importance.

Here are my 14 key professionals that I suggest you have on hand at all times:

1. Coach/Mentor
2. Real Estate Agent/Broker
3. Insurance Agent 4. Accountant
5. Title Agent
6. Certified Home Inspector
7. Good Contractor
8. Handy Man
9. Appraiser
10. Mortgage Banker
11. Private Money lender
12. Property Manager
13. Real Estate Attorney
14. Escrow Closing Agent

Shannon:

How have mentors in your real estate investing helped you navigate potential pitfalls?

Michelle:

A mentor can help you navigate your investment strategies and help you move forward with your career. My mentor is a prime source of support, constructive criticism and unbiased advice, whether I want it or not. He is always there for me when it comes to my investment opportunities.

Shannon:

What advice would you give to someone who is allowing fear to hold them back from starting in real estate investing?

Michelle:

Our minds continuously reinforce the position we take. I believe the key to success is to simply break bad habits/mindsets and replace them with a healthier mindset. I have concluded that the biggest challenge for people wanting to invest is a negative mindset. It sounds like it should be as simple as just switching your perspective, but it's not. They may need to talk to someone about what is actually holding them back.

Shannon:
Is success in real estate investing dependent on a strong economy?

Michelle:
Despite several grossly exaggerated misconceptions, the benefits of real estate investing will play an integral part in returning the housing market to pre-recession standards. As investors, we play a significant role in home appreciation. The acquisition of parcel with intent to restore initiates a process from which the entire neighborhood may benefit. In simple words, no. You can be successful in any market and our current housing market requires us to be successful in a down market.

Shannon:
Can you learn everything you need to know about real estate from the local library?

Michelle:
Absolutely not. You can and should learn everything you need to know from the 14 people I listed above.

Shannon:
What is cash flow and why should it be such an important focus of your business?

Michelle:
Cash flow is of vital importance to the health of your business. If you don't have cash flow, then you don't really have a business, you have a charity. If you have Cash flow you can maintain your business and give back to the community.

Shannon:
Why do people fail at real estate?

Michelle:

I hate the word fail; I don't like to ever use it. I prefer to use the word setback. I believe that lack of knowledge, information, and drive are the only things that prevent success.

Shannon:

Why do people succeed at real estate?

Michelle:

People are successful at real estate because of their hard work, dedication, motivation, and having a good team with the support of their mentors. They have to want it and to set the goals to get there.

Briant &
Jamie Stringham

Briant S. Stringham lll, is an entrepreneur, real estate investor, and owner/ CFO of Business Capital Experts, LLC. His hobbies include spending time with family, traveling with his wife, and playing tennis. As a business owner for over fifteen years, Briant is prolific in helping to build teams, resolve concerns, and create sales teams in multiple states. When not building his business he spends his time mentoring other people who seek to be entrepreneurs through investing in real estate and owning their own businesses.

Jamie Stringham is a professional interior designer, business owner, and entrepreneur. Her company, Interior Dynamics, has been in business since 1988. Jamie has been a real estate investor for the past twenty-six years. She enjoys using her talents as a designer to fix up the properties that she acquires for herself as well as for others. Jamie has ventured into a new online business called DecorEd which offers instruction and interior decorating education for the dabbler. There are also instructional videos to teach real estate marketers tips on making homes more sellable as well as fun ideas and decorating helps.

Contact Info:

Briant Stringham: *Email:* Briant@BusinessCapitalExperts.com
                           Web: www.BusinessCapitalExperts.com
Jamie Stringham, ASID: *Email:* jamie@decoredonline.com
                           Web: www.DecorEDonline.com

Shannon:

According to Forbes Magazine, real estate is one of the top three ways to create wealth. As a real estate investing expert, why do you feel this is the case?

Jamie:

Working a "job" will just make money. It's what you do with that money that can create wealth. Real estate is a great way to make passive income. I am a firm believer in what this Forbes article states: Most money and most wealth is made by investments, not necessarily by an actual job.

Shannon:

What about you Briant?

Briant:

The Forbes article talks about real estate investing allowing people to become wealthy because of leverage. You're able to take a relatively small amount of money and acquire control of a property out of your own or other people's money. The asset grows in value and that's how you become wealthy.

Shannon:

If you're using other people's money, how does that create wealth for you?

Briant:

Simply because with other people's money you're not only going to be paying them a fair return on their investment but also using that money to generate an even bigger return.

Shannon:

Jamie, what is your favorite way to use other people's money? Do you prefer a hard money loan from other people or do you prefer a seller finance?

Jamie:

I personally started investing in properties with my own money and then financed the remainder of the loan; however, having your own money is not necessary. Networking and speaking with other people can be a great way to get started. If you ask enough people eventually you will find someone who is willing to do joint ventures with you. I am a firm believer that you need to talk to everybody you know. You never know who might be interested or know someone that might be looking for an investment. I have a son who is getting into real estate investing with no money. He has had to step out of his comfort zone and network to find the right people that have money to invest with him. My advice is to talk to everybody you know.

Shannon:

How do you approach people to ask if they want to invest with you?

Jamie:

In a typical conversation people will ask, "What do you do?" By letting them know that you invest in real estate, the conversation will generally turn to talking about it. If you talk to enough people, eventually you will find someone who is looking for a place to invest their money.

I believe that it is crucial to be trustworthy. If people can trust you and see that you are educated in real estate, they will feel comfortable investing with you. There are a lot of people that have money sitting in their accounts ready to invest, but they don't have the education to know what to do with it. When you start talking to them often it will spur an idea that they may like to invest.

Shannon:

What kind of events do you go to? Do you go to the Chamber of Commerce, Better Business Bureau, or just a dinner party?

Jamie:

My first and favorite places are private parties and dinner socials. Speaking to established friends and acquaintances is a lot easier than asking a stranger. I do attend "meet ups "with different real estate investing organizations and groups and belong to a group called "The Social Registry." It's an opportunity just to meet people. I can meet people standing in a grocery store line, just by talking.

Shannon:
Briant, do you do that too or is that Jamie's job in your partnership?

Briant:
No, she's the best in whatever she does. I just follow along. When I get talking to people, we get down to brass tacks a little bit. I'll ask them if they've got money in their IRAs or the 401(k)s. Most people do and I ask if they are happy with their return, most say no so I talk to them about the safety and security of real estate, especially when you are educated and know what you're doing.

Some people are interested to learn a little bit more. Then you've got an opportunity to talk to them and show them what can be done. You may not get them first round but you keep them involved. You show them your returns after a deal, and they'll jump in the next time. You just want to make sure that you're a man of your word and that you do what you say you're going to do and people will, as my wife says, "gravitate toward you."

Shannon:
What inspired you to get into real estate?

Jamie:
My parents had real estate investments my entire life. They had single-family homes and multi-family units, as well as commercial real estate. Real estate investing was the talk at our dinner table. When I was about eight, my Dad bought a record that we listened to, "The Richest Man in Babylon" by George S. Clason. From it I learned that 10 percent of all I earn is mine to keep. This was the beginning of setting aside money to be invested.

Shannon:
Did you naturally go into real estate investing, since your dad was in it?

Jamie:
I'm an interior designer, and I own my own design firm in Las Vegas. I started real estate investing right after I was married. We bought our

first home and then began saving and looking for the next one. The next year we bought another property. Each year we would set a goal to invest in more property. It's just what you did with your money.

Shannon:
How long have you two been married?

Jamie:
Briant and I married six years ago in 2010. It has been very natural for me to understand him as a real estate investor. I know of a lot of relationships that struggle because one spouse may have a fear of investing their money. They just want what they think is security. This can be stifling to a relationship. I have not had that fear because of the example of my family.

Shannon:
How long have you been an interior designer?

Jamie:
It's been about thirty-two years.

Shannon:
Does your background in interior design help with your fix and flips?

Jamie:
Absolutely. I use my knowledge all the time.

Briant:
She's good at it too.

Let me tell you about my inspiration for getting involved in real estate. It's similar to Jamie's. My inspiration was my grandfather. He died when he was only sixty-three. Now at the time, he seemed like a real old man because I was only seven or eight, but he instilled in me two goals though I didn't realize it at the time. The first was to own a successful business, as he did, and the second thing was to own property.

He had commercial property, ranching property, and his own

home. He added things on it that I liked, like a tennis court and a basketball court. That inspired me, even though I didn't realize it then but I do now. I'm grateful to my grandfather for the life that he lived and the way that he looked at business and real estate investing.

Shannon:
You said that you didn't realize it at the time, so did you go right into real estate investing?

Briant:
In fact, my father was a little different than my grandfather. My father believed in having a business. That was important, and I was always involved in our family business. He didn't particularly like real estate, especially rental real estate, because he never wanted to be bothered by people calling him because of problems with their property.

He was a little more of a speculator; he would invest in raw land with the hopes that one day it would be worth something. That was his way. I went a little different way. My former spouse, she wanted security. She didn't like the idea of working for yourself and didn't like investing in real estate. After that marriage ended, I was free to do what I wanted, and that's when I purchased my first multifamily property, which I still own to this day.

Shannon:
What advice would you give to someone who is married and one half wants to invest and the other half is saying, "No."

Jamie:
I think that is probably a huge problem in a lot of marriages. There's a lot of frustration for somebody that has an entrepreneurial mindset and they're married to somebody who does not. It's a scary place to be. I think somehow they have to really show their spouse that it can really work. They have to work extra hard and be extra determined to make it happen, to work against the odds.

Sometimes, without any support from a spouse, they just have to jump off the ledge. Go for it and pray that it works, and when it does work out, then they start to develop a little bit more faith, until they finally can convert somebody over to their way of thinking. They have to first have that little bit of success, before the others with join in.

Shannon:
Why are multi-family units a good investment and how do you go about finding these properties?

Briant:
I was very fortunate that the first property that I invested in was a multi-family. My mentality leans a bit toward "buy and hold;" I like to see cash flow; that is really key. That first multi-family, which I still own, cash flowed from day one. It made sense to me and, it was also the place that I lived in right after my divorce.

After the divorce, I did have a little money from our home that I was able to invest in this property. Three years ago I acquired a reverse mortgage on my multi-family; this allowed me to turn my equity into cash for investing while continuing to control the rent in three units. I still keep one unit, so I have a place to live when in Salt Lake. We were also able to help out my sister, as she's able to stay there. It provides us with positive cash flow, and I'm always looking for more of those properties because that was such a great acquisition.

Shannon:
Where do you live right now?

Briant:
We have a home in Las Vegas. My principal residence is Salt Lake.

Shannon:
Do you invest in multi-units in Vegas or just in Salt Lake at this point?

Briant:
Right now, it's in Salt Lake. The market for multi-families here in Vegas is not as good. The rents have not really increased very much over the last twenty years and they just have not been a very good investment.

Unless we find something that really, really makes sense, we don't do a multi-family here in Vegas.

Shannon:

What is cash flow and why is it so important?

Briant:

I always look at a property and determine how much money it is going to bring in on a regular monthly basis, rental income. If all the figures work out and it shows a positive cash flow, (that means it doesn't go negative), then I consider it for acquisition.

Property appreciation is an after effect that can be profitable if one day you decide to sell. Right now, my buy and hold strategy is just that—buy and hold, let it pay for itself. Pay off those mortgages, accelerate that debt pay down, and let that cash flow come in and pad your bank account.

Shannon:

In a single-family home, that seems like it would be pretty easy to do. If your payment is $600 per month and you're renting it for $800, that's positive cash flow, but on the multi-family home, do you have to calculate differently?

Briant:

It depends on how well you buy it. If you could buy a multi-unit, say a four-plex, and know that every month, the nut was taken care of with the rent of just two units and the other two were additional revenue, that's a very good deal. As long as the rent amount that you are collecting is more than the payment and upkeep on the property, that is positive cash flow.

Jamie:

I think that a big advantage to multi-family homes is that, if one unit is not rented, at least there's still some income from the other units that could pay for the mortgage, etc. As opposed to a single-family dwelling where, if they don't pay the rent, then you're totally out of pocket for the entire amount. You have nothing coming in at that point.

Briant:

Good point.

Shannon:

Would you ever invest in a property that does not have positive cash flow for the first year but the next year it would?

Briant:

I probably wouldn't invest in it, unless I have some absolute knowledge that something is going to be different in a year. I won't do it because the figures just don't lie, and I've learned that. Why do something when it's going to cost you money, when you can do something that makes you money?

Shannon:

Jamie, what is your favorite investment strategy right now?

Jamie:

I enjoy doing fix and flips, probably because of my interior design background. It's fun to take something and embellish it into a beautiful property that becomes desirable to a buyer, and then turn around and make the profit at the sell. That's exciting to me. The profit creates leverage to make other purchases. I do believe in buy and hold, that's eventually the ultimate goal, because that's what creates the passive income.

Shannon:

You two are married so you have built-in support. Do you think that people can be just as successful on their own?

Jamie:

A joint venture is a great way to get started as it is helpful to have a partner to help with the decision process. It can also help you to be more courageous. In my former marriage, my husband and I invested together. After we divorced I was single for ten years.

I knew I wanted to invest in real estate, but it was a little scary at first when I was making decisions all alone. I had a girlfriend that was in the same situation, and we pooled our funds together and made several investments. It was really a lot of fun to have somebody else that was equally invested. Together we had courage. We were more powerful together than by ourselves.

Briant and I are of the same mind. I have seen people that become self-educated in real estate investing. It is doable, but to me you make a lot of costly mistakes. I would much rather work with a mentor that has experience that I can learn from. I feel that getting real estate education is essential. I am not a fan of doing it from the library, because I think that a lot of the information there is not always up to date. Finding an organization or a group that has current education and information is way more powerful.

Shannon:
Do you have a support group that you meet with on a regular basis?

Jamie:
Absolutely.

Shannon:
Tell me about the last support group meeting and what came out of it? What was the most creative idea or what was the biggest thing that you learned?

Jamie:
We just had a seminar on debt acceleration. I am excited to put those new skills to work.

Shannon:
Debt acceleration? That does not sound good!

Briant:
We have two huge expenses in life: taxes and interest. When you've got a thirty-year mortgage on a property you pay most of the interest up front. It is called "front-end loading" the mortgage. If you have

a $1200 payment, probably $1,100 of it goes towards interest and less than $100 goes towards the actual principal. You are just paying way too much interest. If you have a way to pay down that mortgage principal quickly, that's going to save you hundreds of thousands of dollars in interest. Also, the quicker you pay your debt off, your cash flow goes up proportionally.

Shannon:

Do you two mentor anyone?

Briant:

Yes, Jamie's son. I invited him to attend a real estate mastermind group, and Jamie is always talking investing with him. Also, we look at deals with other people and talk about what it would take to do them, so in a roundabout way, we are mentors.

Shannon:

When you get that itch to find a new property to invest in, where do you go? How do you find it?

Jamie:

Sometimes I just drive around a neighborhood that I know I want to be in and look for a home that is in distress. You can tell by just looking at the property. In Las Vegas, it's very easy: the plants are all dead; the water is turned off; the swimming pool has turned green. Other parts of the country might be harder to tell, but it's really easy here. The secret is to finding that home right before it actually goes into foreclosure.

I believe keeping your eyes open is very helpful, but I also find that just talking and networking so people know what we're involved in and that we are looking for properties in distress works too. Sometimes you just want to say, "Come and talk to me and we'll talk about the different creative ways that we can help to resolve the problem."

Shannon:

Briant, what about you, do you look for properties the same way?

Briant:

I'm probably a little bigger on the networking side. I just find that by the time they've gone into foreclosure, then you've got your real work cut out because then you're dealing with banks. With networking, people understand that you're an investor and you're not there to take advantage but to actually help them find solutions to their problems.

It may not benefit you on that particular property but when word gets out about you and they know you're sincere and genuine and really do care about helping people, they're going to recommend you.

Shannon:

What if you're just not a social person? Should you not get into real estate investing?

Jamie:

Absolutely not! You can take a different approach. You can go to county records to find information, people that are going through divorce or who've had a death in the family. Send out letters to show you are interested in their property. There are different ways that you can go about finding properties. You need to figure out which way will work best for you. For me, talking to people is much easier, probably because I am so social. It's a lot more fun.

Shannon:

Can anybody go down to county records and look them up or do you have to pay some sort of fee?

Jamie:

Anybody can go down and do the work. There is no charge, but it takes real determination. If you're just dabbling, it just doesn't really happen. Instead, I think it's a lot about your persistence.

My son, for instance, has spent time going through public records. He has sent out letters and knocked on several doors. He will succeed in this business, because he is determined to do so.

Shannon:
Is it appropriate to use a short sale strategy for the homes that you find at the county records?

Briant:
Basically, a short sale is a bit of a misnomer because I've never seen a short sale that was short in duration. Typically, a short sale is at the point where it's gone, or about to go, into foreclosure so it takes more time and more effort but it can be very, very profitable. I have a mentor that has short sales as his area of expertise, and he is very good at dealing with the banks.

Shannon:
Do you know of a strategy that you have never used but are really excited to try?

Briant:
Yes, in fact, I've discussed this many times with a good friend and associate—flipping hotels. Hotels can get into trouble just like any other property. In fact, he's on-site right now acquiring a hotel for a fix and flip. It will take a little longer, probably a two-year time frame, but the amount of money they look to make is substantial.

Shannon:
Jamie, are there any real estate strategies that you have learned about but not yet tried that you are excited to do?

Jamie:
I would have to say that I am excited to partner with Briant. I'm excited about the idea of getting involved with the hotels and a little bit more on a commercial side.

Briant:
For Jamie, with her interior design and specialization in commercial space, it's a natural for us. That's one that we're educating ourselves on right now. It looks to us to be really a great strategy. We're excited about it. That's where our efforts are going right now.

Shannon:

What is the legacy that you hope to leave behind?

Jamie:

It's important to me to teach my family and encourage them to become educated in real estate investing. I don't want to just leave them with my investments, but I want to leave them with the education to manage those investments. I would like to watch them make their own investments as well. That to me would be a true legacy.

I appreciate that my parents left me with great examples, and their legacy continues on because of the education that they taught. This is what I would hope to do for my family.

Briant:

The only legacy that I hope to pass on is a living legacy. I don't want it to be a hand out. I want to instill in them the concept that they will succeed if they apply education along with a conviction to use their brains and never give up. I want them to compound the legacy that I leave so that it truly goes on and on and benefits each succeeding generation.

The principles I believe in are true principles, and they will continue. I don't want anybody to figure it's a free ride because it's not. I want them to go to work and do more and build more and make it grow.

Tim Vreeland

Tim Vreeland is an award-winning Real Estate Investor and Entrepreneur and has been recognized across the nation for his achievements in real estate and debt reduction strategies. He received a bachelor's degree from Brigham Young University, Hawaii, and worked for one of the largest accounting firms, nutraceutical companies, and brokerage firms before transitioning into real estate investing. He has a high level of commitment to his real estate education, and has been mentored and coached by several of the most highly acclaimed real estate coaches in the industry. He now assists others in overcoming barriers and achieving great results in real estate investing.

Contact Info:
Web: www.vreelandrealestate.com

Shannon:
What inspired you to get into real estate?

Tim:
In a nutshell, family. I knew from a young age that not only did I want to be an entrepreneur like my father, but that I wanted to surpass him. I remember him working full-time as a furniture salesman and then having a side-business running a travel agency from home. There would be travel magazines all over the house and a designated phone line for any customers that call. It never really went anywhere, though. In fact, looking back now, it looks like he never got out of start-up mode. He also tried his luck taking over a sandwich shop, which ended in disaster, but the important lesson that stuck to me was that my father had the entrepreneurial spirit in him and I knew he tried his best at creating a legacy his family can follow, and as time went on, I felt like I wanted to see my father's wishes through.

The important thing that one needs to know in order to be an entrepreneur is knowing what you are good at. As I was going through college and trying to figure out what I was passionate about, I discovered that I loved to find solutions to complex problems. When I was looking at all the different avenues of where that would be best applied, I thought about having a long tenured career in operations management, working for a large international company, and eventually becoming a Chief Operation Officer (COO). Right after I graduated from college, though, I found myself unemployed in a world-wide hiring freeze. I even went door-to-door to different businesses with my resume in hand asking for work, to no avail. During my job search, my older sister, who was an active real estate agent at the time, talked to me about how lucrative investing in real estate could be. She said she heard that there were ways to buy properties creatively, but she didn't know how. That intrigued me and planted a seed of interest in my mind. Shortly after, however, I found work through a temp service as a machine operator at a manufacturing facility. I figured that was my foot in the door toward my long term goal of becoming a COO.

Just after being hired, my brother, who was involved in a real estate community at the time, invited me to go to a real estate meeting with a mentor of his. I didn't know what to expect at that meeting, but the things that were presented rang true to me. At that event I met a seasoned real estate investor who shared with me a time when he helped a homeowner out of a bad situation. The homeowner had lost his job and the bank was about to foreclose on his house. The real estate investor was able to step in and stop the foreclosure process! He successfully negotiated a short sale with the bank that let the homeowner walk away free and clear from his house. What that investor did was something I never knew was possible... He created a win/win/win solution; a win for the homeowner because he avoided foreclosure on his credit and could walk away free and clear of any mortgage debt, a win for the bank because the bank was able to get a bad performing asset off their books, and a win for the investor because he made over $20,000 in one month! After I heard that story a lightbulb turned on in my mind. Real estate investors not only make money doing what they do, they solve problems where traditional means cannot! I saw a glimpse into my future of what becoming a real estate investor would do for me and my family, and the tremendous value I would be able to provide to the world. I could see myself being the husband and father I was aspiring to be. I saw myself having the means and time available to give the meaningful service I wanted to give. I knew that I would be able to leave a legacy that would change the course of my family for years to come.

So my initial reason of wanting to get involved in real estate was a shallow and selfish reason for just making money, evolved into a greater cause to help those in need by using my passion to solve problems. My goal in life became to create value in the marketplace by helping anyone overcome their real estate challenges. None of this would have been possible if it wasn't for the experiences my family members gave to me growing up.

Shannon:
How was it a win/win/win? The homeowner is losing their home. It seems that there are only two wins.

Tim:

If someone is about to lose their home due to losing their job, going through a divorce, or because of medical issues, the worst thing they can ever do is lose their house through foreclosure. Nobody wins in that scenario. The homeowner gets a huge penalty on their credit that would prevent them from buying a new house anytime soon. The bank doesn't want to take back a home. That will look bad on their books and actually decreases the amount they are able to lend out according to federal regulations.

Nobody should ever have to lose their home like that. The win for a homeowner in working with me is that I actually tell them all their options, not just the one that makes me money. My philosophy is that if you are going to create value in someone's life and guide them towards the best solution to their problem, then they need to know all their options. The sooner they act, the sooner they can move on to the next chapter of their life. The benefit with working with me is that a homeowner can get immediate relief from their issues because they have a buyer sitting right in front of them, ready to act quickly and make that headache go away. Do you know how satisfying it is to see the look on someone's face when they first learn that they don't need to lose their house and they actually have options? It's what drives me to do what I do!

Avoiding a foreclosure is the best thing for anybody. There are better solutions than allowing their home to be taken.

Shannon:

Is there such a thing as it being too late to avoid the foreclosure?

Tim:

The only time that it's too late is when your house goes to auction and the auctioneer says "sold!"

Shannon:

Do the banks do that because in the long run it's actually better for them than going to auction?

Tim:

Absolutely! Banks would rather avoid foreclosing on people's' homes, but they have to do something to protect their interests and investments. If banks end up foreclosing on someone and take back the property, a few negative things follow: that house will deteriorate over time as most homes just sit there from one to five years until they are listed again, the banks have to put more money into maintaining and repairing that vacant property until they find another buyer, and most importantly in the eyes of the bank, having a "bad asset" on their books restricts how much money they are able to loan out. It is in the bank's best interest to get rid of the house as quick as possible. A real estate investor, like myself, can help the bank remedy that.

Shannon:

What if the bank is firm on a price that is too high?

Tim:

It has to be a win for all parties in order for me to do a deal. If I don't get the price that makes sense for me to take on the risks that come with buying a home, then it's no deal. I have to buy at a price that makes sense. There has to be enough profit in there to protect me from unforeseen problems. The price of homes will always fluctuate from year to year and I have never been a part of a rehab project that never ended up having unplanned repair costs. I try to be there at every stage of a short sale in order to ensure that the bank understands the fair market value of the house. That's why I put so much time and energy into analyzing the house and looking for those unforeseen costs. When I am involved in negotiating with the banks from the start, I usually get the price I need to make it a win for me.

Shannon:

Do you need to have a realtor's license to be a good investor?

Tim:

Having a Realtor's license certainly has its perks, but the truth is, no one needs a license to start investing in real estate. There are pros and cons to getting a realtor's license. If you have your realtor's license it's another arrow in your quiver to take down deals and help people out, but it also adds costs. A realtor needs to be tied to a brokerage firm and has to pay all sorts of fees to keep licensed. For me, the only reason to get one is to gain access to the MLS. With real estate, time is of the essence and if there is a house that actually qualifies as a good deal on the MLS, then it is either gone by the end of the day or has multiple offers. If I need to access to the MLS, I ask one of the realtors I work with to help me.

Real estate is not a solo game. It takes a team to make it happen. I just make sure I have some good realtors on my sidelines who can quickly get back to me.

Shannon:
What are some creative ways to look for a home to invest in?

Tim:
The best way is by word of mouth. People have to know you are an investor looking for properties, so open up your mouth. Your friends and neighbors know you best and are able to break through the trust barrier a lot quicker than you can by cold calling. Other ways to find homes is by marketing to homeowners who show up on the county recorder's Notice of Default list. They're good candidates who may be open to creative ways of selling their property. If you're trying to market to them, send them postcards, knock on their doors, put up "I buy houses" signs around the neighborhood, anything you can do to start up a conversation with the homeowner.

I've knocked on hundreds of doors to let the homeowners know that I am just a guy looking for a house to buy. I ask questions because the more I know about their situation the better I can come up with a win-win scenario. I can tell if the homeowner is ready to work with me by the way they answer those questions. Listening to their answers is crucial since they don't usually disclose that they are behind on their mortgage payment. As I ask them deeper questions about the balance on their mortgage, what their payments are, and if they are current, I can get a better feel for their willingness to work with me.

When I send mailers to people who show up on the NOD list, the postcards say, "My wife and I would like to buy your house. Give us a call. Have a good day." To be respectful, I avoid any wording that lets them think I know they are going through a tough time. Nothing I've sent would ever say, "Hey you, avoid foreclosure!." These home-owners are already going through a tough time and I don't want to be just another person bombarding them.

Shannon:
How has education changed the way you invest?

Tim:
At my earliest stage of aspiring to get into real estate I tried to be cheap and do it the "free" way, because my naive mind thought, "I'm smart enough, I got my degree, I can go and try to figure out a way to do real estate investing myself." 2 years of thinking that way didn't prove to be fruitful. I read books on investing, but I felt that I wasn't getting up-to-date information nor did I feel adequate or prepared enough to follow through with what I was reading. I went to various real estate association meetings which cost anywhere from $100 to $250 each and were filled with professionals and people looking to make money, but they weren't willing to take aspiring beginners by the hand to show them the road to true real estate investing. In fact, not much of them had a true grasp of what being a true investor was all about. After two years of investigating, I had not done a single deal. I understood that I needed to be taken by the hand and mentored by someone I could trust to keep me out of trouble and to keep me from being taken advantage of. This is where the real estate group that my brother introduced me to comes into play.

3 months after joining, I had found my first fix and flip property and made $15,000. What I learned from my ordeals is that if anyone wants to achieve anything in life, they must first surround themselves with people who have already achieved your aspiration. Through this real estate group, I had the support, the education, and the mentorship to push through the fears and barriers that were holding me back.

Shannon:

How have some of your mentors in real estate investing helped you to navigate potential pitfalls?

Tim:

The biggest thing that impressed me was that before I joined my brother's real estate group, my brother's mentor would answer all my phone calls and help me with my questions. I would call him at all hours of the day and ask him for his advice on many things, including potential deals that were presented to me by various real estate investors and realtors. The investors were just looking to unload their bad inventory and most realtors didn't know how to run numbers like an investor. I was naïve and trusting of those investors and thought that they had my best interests at heart. When I would call a mentor in my brother's real estate group, he would crunch numbers with me and almost every time would say, "Whoa, Tim, that's not a good deal. They're just trying to unload their bad deals on you. Let's get educated and find real deals." I was taught that you make your money in real estate when you buy it. If you buy it wrong, then you will either lose money on the deal or you will be holding onto it for years and years in hopes that time will raise the equity of the home, which tactic ties up your money and holds you back from doing more deals and purchasing more properties.

Buying at the wrong price is really a rookie mistake.

When you watch shows on HDTV go over their numbers, they make it sound so easy, but they aren't showing the viewers about all the other costs. There are closing costs that come out between 3-5% on the buying end, and 3-5% on the selling end. There are realtor fees if you list it, which typically come to 6% in my area when you sell. Those two costs can equate to around 30-40K right there. So when I hear someone telling me that they can buy a property for 150K and sell it for 200K, I already know that they are looking to lose 30-50K even before getting started.

Then there are the costs to borrow the money needed to purchase the property and fund the rehab. This is usually done through a money lender, and traditionally real estate investors will use hard money lenders.

Shannon:

What's a hard money lender?

Tim:

A hard money lender is somebody who's willing to finance most of the acquisition of a home and the rehab, but they expect to get their money back quickly, typically between six months to a year. Some hard money lenders want to have the investor put some skin in the game and pay 10-20% of the purchase price. Most of them expect to be paid points up front too, which is an up-front fixed fee based on the amount of money they lend out. They may also expect monthly interest-only payments. They're expensive, but if you don't have the money, then they are a great tool to leverage to take down more properties without having to use your own money. This is why it is so important to make sure there is enough profit in the deal to make it worthwhile.

Shannon:

Do they offer a higher interest rate or lower interest rate than a standard bank loan?

Tim:

Banks have a record of being cheaper to borrow, but the time it takes to approve a loan is daunting. The great incentive of having home owners work with an investor is the ability to close quickly. Traditional financing defeats the purpose of a fast close. Hard Money Lenders are typically fast a lending the funds and don't look at the investor as much as they do the deal. These lenders want to make sure their money is protected, and if they can see a good profit, then the funds to purchase a property can come out as quickly as 1-3 days or as long as 2 weeks. When it comes to cost to use hard money, it depends on the lender, their terms, and how much they are lending out. Typically, I have seen 1-3 points upfront and then 10-12% APY. I have had a money lender lend every dollar needed to complete a project, from start to finish, but it wasn't cheap.

Because it is a little costly to use hard money, it gives you incentive to finish your rehab quickly, or to refinance into a better term loan quickly. The worst case scenario when using hard money is losing the property. The lender usually does their analysis beforehand and feels comfortable that they are protected in case that happens and will be able to get their money back. If you decide to use a hard money lender in your deal, you'd better be certain that you're going to make money and you're going to meet your deadlines.

Shannon:
Do you find that most of the people that you have these relationships with are understanding if you're a month or two behind your schedule?

Tim:
Most of the time there are penalties already built in place for extending a month or two or even a year, but It does depend on how good of a relationship you have with your money lender. You've got to show up as competent, and you have to be professional. Professionals keep their word, so it's better to foresee issues before you get started and negotiate more time into your deal beforehand. If you run out of time and you have to pay them back, what's your backup plan? Are you able to bring in another money partner to pay off your hard money lenders to make everyone happy? Sometimes problems do arise and you may need to negotiate more time with your lenders and they will be fine with the extensions. In my experience, money lenders are not in business to set up investors to fail. They would rather see you succeed and make money than take a property from you.

Shannon:
What do you think is the number one mistake that an individual makes when buying their first investment property?

Tim:
To me, there are two big mistakes: First is undertaking a deal uneducated thinking you can wing it and expect to make money. Those are the people who buy properties at 150k thinking they can sell for 200k and make a profit. What you don't know really can hurt you. The other mistake is thinking you can do it alone.

Shannon:
Have you ever seen anyone be successful doing it alone?

Tim:
In my experience, no. If you are looking to make real estate a way to make extra money and a great career, then you are kidding yourself if you think that you can do it alone. Maybe you can buy your own house, fix it up, sell it for a profit and then move into another home right after, but how many times can someone do that in their lifetime? 3-5 times? That isn't real estate investing. In real estate, what you don't know really can hurt you and can cost you greatly! Think about it this way: People can do their taxes themselves each year. They don't need to hire a CPA. People don't need a lawyer to represent them in court. Why do we still hire CPAs and lawyers? We do this because they are the professionals and know much more in their respective fields than we do. My CPA has taken the time to educate himself in the best tax strategies real estate investors can use to minimize their taxes. Wouldn't someone rather pay a few hundred dollars for that kind of expertise that can save them tens of thousands of dollars each year, or would they rather keep their money to themselves and use some online software that doesn't have the intuition to use tax code to your advantage, ultimately costing you tens of thousands of dollars. You are only as strong as the people you surround yourself with.

In another sense, would you like somebody to perform surgery on you if all they did was read books on how to perform it and say, "How hard could it be?" Or how about one of your buddies, after attending a three-day boot camp on flying airplanes, comes up to you and asks, "Hey, want to come fly with me? Don't worry, I know what I'm doing!"?

Shannon:
No! I don't want to be on their airplane or operating table.

Tim:
Everyone should feel the same with real estate! You need to have the right attorneys, the right title agents, the right realtors, the right

mentors, the right contractors, the right money lenders, and the right partners in place in order to do a successful deal. I have never seen an investor succeed by their own efforts alone. You also have to make sure that the people you are bringing on to your team understand and share your vision and be on board with the way you do business.

Shannon:
What is your favorite exit strategy?

Tim:
Well, my two favorite exit strategies are fix and flip or buy and hold. Fix and flip, of course, is where you make the most money upfront. You buy a home, you buy it low, you fix it up and you sell it for the best price you can. That's great, because it's very lucrative. The downside is that you need to be out there constantly find deals to flip if or else you run out of money eventually. In that strategy, you only make money if you work, so if anything happens to you, then there goes your stream of money.

Once you close on a deal, you would typically make between 20-50K. Four to six months is a long time to wait, so you had better be working on a few properties at a time in order to make it sustainable. This is considered "massive income."

A successful real estate investor needs to also incorporate a buy and hold strategy. This creates steady or "passive income." The more rentals you have that create positive cash flow, the more freedom you can create for yourself. It's just a matter of being a solution to people's problems. Half my rental portfolio was created by purchasing homes subject to the existing mortgage staying in place. In order for that strategy to work, there needs to be a good positive cash flow after all expenses.

Think of it like the legs of a chair. Most chairs have four legs. If one leg gets kicked off, the other legs can still support you. If all you do is focus on one income stream in real estate, then when the economy, or life, kicks that one leg from under you, you fall hard. A flip gives you your massive income and the rental gives you the passive income you need to retire and walk away from your job, or to step away from working to spend time with your family and enrich your life. I've only talked about two streams of income. There are others, but those are my favorite.

Shannon:
Do you have a long term goal for how many properties you want to own?

Tim:
My long term goal is to control 100 rental properties paying for themselves and generate a net cash flow of $10,000. At that stage, I will be in a situation where I can truly retire if I choose to. Since I love what I do so much, I can see myself spending my time helping others get into real estate investing the right way.

Shannon:
How is that going to create passive income if you're having to manage all of those rental properties?

Tim:
When you're an investor, you don't have time to be a full-time landlord and go over to a unit at all hours of the day, unclogging toilets or changing light bulbs. You need to be free to find more deals. This is where finding the right property manager becomes very important.

Shannon:
Do you think a successful real estate investor, with a buy and hold strategy should invest only locally, or invest in other areas of the nation?

Tim:
Right now, I focus on my local market. It's easier to control properties when they are within a 30-minute drive, as opposed to putting my trust in a management company I barely know to manage a property I would need to fly or drive a long way to, in order to ensure everything is running okay. When I find the right partners that I trust in other states, then they will definitely be my feet on the ground and I will feel more comfortable owning properties outside of my local market.

Shannon:

What do you want your legacy to look like?

Tim:

I'm paving the way for my children to be able to create wealth and freedom in their lives. I am creating a life where my family and kids live the life that they want while sharing it with others.

I come from a family of humble circumstances with a hard working mentality where they trade their time for dollars. After watching the example of my father trying to break free of that paradigm by trying to create his own businesses and being an entrepreneur, it has inspired me to want to carry out my father's dream. I want to instill upon my children an abundance mentality and a wealthy mindset. Whether or not they feel that real estate's the path for them, I created an environment that will cultivate their entrepreneurial spirits so they can go out and have a positive impact on the world. I want to give them the means to pursue their dreams.

Our time is precious and finite. We only have so much. Money is abundant and there doesn't seem to be an end to that resource. Money should be used as a tool to enrich our lives and to give us more time to spend on things that truly matter, like family, and making the world a better place.

Perran & Loretta Wetzel

Perran Wetzel IV is President of PG Wetzel and Associates, Inc. and Loretta Dooley Wetzel is President of The Wetzel Group, Inc. both of Chicago, Illinois. Perran is an accomplished, top-performing accounting professional and business owner with diversified experience in accounting, business management, tax, audit, review, compilation, and business valuation with an emphasis on entrepreneurs and small to medium-sized companies. He received his BA in Accounting from Luther College, Decorah, Iowa, and is a member of good standing in the National Society of Accountants and National Society of Tax Preparers.

Loretta is an accomplished and professional real estate investor, mentor, coach, trainer, and speaker. She is also an International Certified Coach for John C. Maxwell and currently has her own real estate investing and financial literacy talk radio show, "Keepin' It Real with Lori Wetzel," on the Voice America business channel where she will create an "I can do it too" attitude for entrepreneurial success. She received her MBA from the University of Illinois.

Both Perran and Loretta are Founders Advisory Board Members for Renatus, LLC, an education company for real estate investors.

Contact Info:
Perran Guy Wetzel IV: *Email:* perran@pgwetzel.com
Loretta Dooley Wetzel: *Email:* info@thewetzelgroup.com

Shannon:

What inspired you to get into real estate?

Loretta:

I actually spent most of my professional career in non-profit and for-profit corporations. My last corporate job was in the airline industry employed as a senior human resource manager supervising over a hundred staff members at the employee contact center, they paid me very well. I earned over six figures at that company, plus benefits. I worked the typical 'corporate America' job, meaning I worked more than forty hours a week. I didn't get paid overtime being classified as an exempt employee. Sometimes, I would work weekends to catch up or whatever it took until the job was done to meet deadlines. I missed a lot of my kids' extracurricular activities but I thought, "They are paying me a nice salary, suck it up."

The work schedule was brutal. I had an hour-and-fifteen-minute commute each way on a good weather day, thirty-six miles one way with guaranteed traffic. On a bad weather day, it could take me three or four hours to get home, especially if there was snow since we lived in Chicago. I was expected to be back to work the next day on time, and I also expected employees reporting to me to do the same.

In April of 2010, plans were underway for the completion of an airline merger. Now everybody knows what happens when two big companies come together—corporations must trim the expenses. Suddenly, I found myself laid off from my six-figure income position—plus, I like to say I am blessed with age (being over fifty)—and we had two kids in college at the time with out-of-state tuition. I was terrified because all I knew was to get up and go to work in a cubicle. My parents instilled in me a strong work ethic, but I knew it was going to be tough to find a job to replace the income I was used to earning. Fortunately, the seeds of entrepreneurship were planted by my parents early in life, and I didn't even realize it.

My Dad worked at the post office, and he also ran a newspaper distributorship. He was responsible for making sure we received The Daily News newspapers and then they were delivered by the paperboys to our customers. The seed of entrepreneurship was planted because I saw my Dad work the night shift at the post office, come home, get a couple of hours of sleep, get up, and then he would work his own business. We all had chores growing up and everybody had at least one night of the week to cook dinner. We all washed our own clothes and still had time for piano lessons. Work ethic, as well as family time, was important. Thank you Daddy for instilling in me my love of travel, teaching me how to play chess, and how to change a flat tire. In those days, girls didn't do that, but my father taught me the value of these skills. Thank you Mom for instilling self-confidence in me and my love of reading books. My Mom ALWAYS told me I could do and be whatever I wanted in life, and she prepared me that it would be a tough road ahead. "Loretta," she would say, "you are a girl and a Negro (this was before the popular James Brown song, 'Say it Loud! I'm Black and I'm Proud') so society will count two strikes against you. If everybody else in your class is receiving a B grade, you had better get an A. If everybody else is receiving an A grade, you had better get an A+." At that young age, I didn't know what a glass ceiling was, but my Mom in her wisdom prepared me well for the future. To this day, I still smile on the inside when people underestimate me. We also didn't have a lot of extra money growing up, but whenever I wanted a new book, there was no pushback. Besides, I had smoke rising from my library card due to the usage, and soon the library in my disadvantaged neighborhood couldn't keep up with my voracious reading appetite. One night, I sneaked a flashlight into my bedroom at night so I could continue reading *Watership Down* by Richard Adams. I couldn't put the book down. In short, leaders are readers. Thank you Mom and Dad, you were the best parents for me!

Continuing my entrepreneurial training as a kid, I always wanted a paper route. But my Dad said, "No, it's too dangerous for you. Your brothers can have the paper route." I was bummed out about that because I felt like, "You are discriminating between my brothers and me," but I didn't understand at the time the paperboys collected cash for people to pay their invoice. There were criminal elements out there where the paperboys could get robbed. My Dad obviously was attempting to keep me safe. So I helped my Mom with the book-keeping. That was my job. I became very adept at a ten-key adding machine (this was before the calculator) to balance the books. The money that was collected from the paper route had to be prepared in wrappers for the bank deposits. It was my job to put the quarters, dimes and nickels in the coin wrappers.

I handled all the change and my Dad handled all the dollar bills. He then took the money to the bank. The seeds were planted that banks were for deposits, not withdrawals. I experienced firsthand growing up being an entrepreneur. My job was to stuff the comics and any other inserts into the newspapers every Saturday morning at 6:30 am before I could watch cartoons. That was my job. I couldn't watch cartoons until the job was complete. That was a very valuable lesson for me; work first, play second.

Fast forward to April 2010, I was laid off from my job. I dusted off my resume and I said, "no worries, I've got enough job experience, I have a college degree and an MBA degree so I can find a good paying job." I began to hit the networking circuit. I talked to people, passed out resumes, attended networking events, and received job interviews. I also received job offers. The most anyone offered me was half of my six-figure income for employment. I was at a crossroads when I knew that I had to choose something different for my life. I met a young lady named Jill at a networking event and she said, "Are you open to a business opportunity?" That was all she said to me, the question that changed my life.

Shannon:
That was it?

Loretta:
Yes, that was it! When Jill asked me this question, she looked me dead in the eye. I looked at her and I paused. A little birdie in the back of my mind said, "Choose different." I said, "You know what, I think it's time for me to check out this opportunity." I went home and told my husband. I said, "Honey, I think we should go to this informational meeting. We can see what they have to offer." At the end of the first meeting, we looked at each other knowingly and I said, "This is it. This is what I'm meant to do moving forward. This is an opportunity for us to control our destiny and not be at the whim of major corporations who frankly cared only about their bottom line and nothing else."

We did our due diligence, asked questions; we attended another meeting to check everything out, to make sure it was okay, and then we made a choice. We said we wanted in because I knew that I could bet on me. I wouldn't bet on the corporations, but I knew that I could bet on me and get a return on my investment.

Shannon:
How has your education in real estate investing changed your life?

Loretta:
We began taking the online real estate investing education. That was my new job, so I spent eight hours a day / five days a week soaking in the new information. Two months later, we had our first real estate deal underneath our belt. It was a subject-to exit strategy combined with a fix and flip. The first real estate deal was a little unusual in a sense that this deal was in the state of California and our headquarters are in Illinois. People told us that we could not make money with this deal because we were in the height of the recession or depression, whichever one you want to call it. Yet, our real estate education taught us we could make money on this deal. There was a ton of equity in the property, and we were able to leverage resources. I was in Illinois, but I had access to all the resources I needed within our nationwide real estate investing community. We used a California law firm specializing in working with small businesses. One phone call and twenty-four hours later, we had the #2 broker with Keller-Williams in the area for our property in California.

I was able to use private money from another corporation within the real estate investing community for adding value to the property. Everything I needed based on taking the real estate education, I was able to do it. Four months later, we exited out of that strategy with a nice $80,000 net profit on that first real estate deal.

Shannon:
Perran, before you share your story, I would like know what you were thinking when she looked over to you and said, "This is it."?

Perran:
You have to remember that I have never had a "job" in my entire life. It was nothing new to me about going into business. I'm a risk

taker. When an opportunity arises, I'm the one to go to and take a chance. It was okay with me. I didn't see the problem with it and also the fact that I didn't want her to go back working for somebody else. That was a major factor for me. When she lost her job, it wasn't a big deal to me. I knew that everything was going to be okay because I've been in business my whole adult life, and I know what it takes to be successful. I've been managing my own accounting practice for the last thirty-seven years now. One of the things that it afforded me to do is to check out different opportunities. I've been involved in at least thirty or forty different business opportunities. They may have made money, but never fit with what exactly I wanted to do.

I was always looking for something. When we found real estate investing, it was exactly what we were looking for because it provided us with a team of people and a community to plug into for support. That was missing in all of my opportunities, I didn't have the right team. Get the right team and it makes sense.

Shannon:

If you had found this real estate education and, Loretta, you had not lost your job, do you think you would be doing real estate investing right now?

Loretta:

I say yes, he says no.

Shannon:

Why no?

Perran:

Why no? Due to her job. If you think about it, Loretta would leave the house by 6:30 am and wasn't coming home till 7 or 8 pm in the evening. Consequently, she wouldn't have had the time to invest in the business. Besides, I already have a number of active businesses. We wouldn't have had the time as far as meetings every Thursday. Plus, we host our own Wednesday meetings. We have all these different activities going on, and she wouldn't have been able to participate in most of those activities. I would have been doing them alone.

Loretta:

I've got to admit, Shannon, that's true because I never really envisioned leaving that particular airline company for different employment. I had been with them for fifteen years. Everything is about seniority in the airline industry. It's quite common for people to be in the airline industry for forty or fifty years, straight from high school; it's all they ever know. I didn't really think that I would work anywhere else other than that company. I was surprised that the layoff occurred and yet part of me, as I look back, says I knew that I was meant to do something different, to contribute to others in this world. What I was doing at that job wasn't enough. It just wasn't enough.

Shannon:

I love that you admitted that because I was waiting to hear you say, "No, he's right. I'd still be at the airline." It sounds like you really enjoyed that job other than the commute and that it was comfortable for you.

Loretta:

I enjoyed the people at the job but, to be honest with you, I did not necessarily enjoy the job. I enjoyed making it a fun place to work as much as I possibly could. At the same time, being in human resources is very policy driven. There were times when I had to execute some decisions that I was not comfortable with. As you separate people from employment, for whatever reason, sometimes it's justifiable, sometimes questionable, but in human resources you go by the letter of the law. There are policies and procedures with minimum room for differing interpretations. In HR, you are the bearer of that. You execute your job.

Shannon:

Perran, who inspired you to be an entrepreneur rather than just going straight into corporate America?

Perran:

My father was an entrepreneur as well. Matter of fact, he owned a school bus company called Wetzel Transportation. My Dad Harold was one of the first Black-owned bus companies to have a school bus contract with the City of Chicago Board of Education. He had been in business since 1968. When I graduated from college, my Dad invited me to join the business. I accepted. However, when you have strong-willed people together in a business environment, we did not work too well together. He had his idea about running a business, and I had my idea about running the business. We split up about a year and a half after I graduated. That's when I started my accounting practice and went full-time with my own business.

Shannon:
Where did you go to college?

Perran:
I went to Luther College in Decorah, Iowa. That's where we met, in college. I graduated in 1979, and she graduated the year after that. We were married less than thirty days later after Loretta graduated from college.

Loretta:
I told him that I did not go to school to get my 'MRS' degree and if he really loved me, I had to get my degree first, before I became married. Here is the other thing that is a little unusual with me; I did not graduate from high school. My parents saw in elementary school that I was becoming bored very quickly. My personality is such that I'm not a trouble maker, but I was starting to get in trouble at school. They were wise enough to know it was due to the Chicago public school system that was not challenging enough for me to keep my attention. My parents were able to receive financial aid so I could attend the University of Chicago Laboratory School, a private high school in Chicago. Perran attended Campion Jesuit High School in Prairie du Chien, Wisconsin, an elite boarding school especially for middle-class African American boys whose parents were doctors, lawyers, and politicians.

However, I only attended high school for three and a half semesters. I did not graduate from high school. I went ahead and accepted early admission into college. In my senior year of high school, rather than enjoying prom and senior festivities, in January I attended Luther

College arrived mid-year. I believed I had to get my college degree because I officially did not receive a high school degree.

Shannon:

When doing a short sale, what should you anticipate and how long do they usually take from beginning to end?

Loretta:

We have a running joke in our real estate investment community: there is nothing short about a short sale. They can average anywhere between nine to eighteen months. It just really depends on the lender and who you are working with. You really use your negotiation skills with a short sale. The lender or the current mortgage holder will repeatedly ask for many of the same documents over and over again to be submitted over a period of time. They just want to make sure that the data is up to date and current. Also with the short sale, you really want to make sure that the homeowner who has requested the short sale has a hardship letter that is handwritten and not typed out on a computer. With a handwritten letter and a personal signature explaining why they no longer can afford the property, if the property owner changes his or her mind for what-ever reason, you want to avoid any claims of coercion or accusations that someone forced them to give up their property.

Perran:

Now most of the short sales today are controlled by the realtors. The bank requires the information to be submitted through different software packages. One of the most popular software programs is called Equator. All the documents must be uploaded to that system so you don't really have as much control over the deal. However, not all short sales go through Equator. The deals where you work directly with the homeowner and the mortgage holder without using Equator work best for flexibility and negotiations.

Shannon:

Do you still use the short sale acquisition strategy, or is that a strategy of the past?

Loretta:

It's all about context and how you look at things. I wouldn't necessarily say that it's in the past. One of the nice things about short sales is that you can have income for the future. If you could work the short sale deal and meet all of the requirements, you are going to have future income. You also want to address the deficiency clause in the deal with the agreement that the mortgage holder will not directly go after the homeowner for the difference between the short sale amount and the full amount of the loan.

Perran:

Right, the mortgage holder won't come after the owner upon completion of the short sale.

Shannon:

Is successful investing dependent on a strong economy?

Loretta:

Real estate education allows you to have access to all the tools in the tool kit. You'll have access to multiple acquisition, funding, and exit strategies. Depending upon the deal that comes across your plate, and the factors of the deal, whether the economy is up, down, sideways it really doesn't matter because our education teaches you how to successfully execute the deal (or not) under any environment or conditions.

You can apply these strategies where you see fit. The education teaches you how to analyze deals and then you use the strategy that best fits that particular situation so that you can always make money in real estate. It doesn't matter what the economy is like; it doesn't matter who is in political office; all you need to know is to be educated so you know how to execute the appropriate exit strategies for your deal in order to make money. Then, you must take action and duplicate your success.

Shannon:

Do you two have a favorite strategy or a strategy that you see working best for 2016?

Loretta:

I would say that it's a combination. We call it short-term and long-term strategies. With short-term strategies, it's twelve months or less and typically you are talking about generating massive income. Massive income is when you are paid one time on that asset. It's usually a larger check. Our real estate education has helped us to analyze deals and build in a profit where we do that analysis. It minimizes the risk of losing money. You don't want to ever lose money in real estate. You may not make as much money as you thought you were going to make, but you don't ever want to lose money on a real estate deal; that's the key to being educated.

The key to becoming wealthy is executing long term strategies to generate passive income. You want to buy and hold onto properties and be able to generate passive income whether you work or not. You don't ever want to be tied to what we call linear income, which is trading time for dollars; this is what you do in corporate America or any job. To be able to combine the two strategies I believe works best. Perran, do you have anything you want to add?

Perran:

My particular strategy is that I like three-unit buildings for the fact that one of the units pays for the mortgage, one of the units pays for any rehab the property needs, and the third unit pays for all your profits. If one of the units is vacant, or even two of the units are vacant, the property can still pay for itself. That's something that I like. Some people like single-family houses, other people like apartment buildings, but that's one of the things that I like.

Shannon:

If someone is willing to invest in a multi-family dwelling, what is the first thing that you will tell them they need to know?

Perran:

The most important thing to understand with your investment is your risk tolerance. That's the most important thing, understanding who you are. We have a class called "Understanding your Investor

ID." If you're not quite sure what type of investor you are and the type of properties you want to invest in, understanding what your ID is before you invest in anything is a critical step.

Loretta:

The other thing with the multi-family dwelling is the calculations are different than if you are purchasing a single-family residence. In multi-family dwellings, you are looking at something called the capitalization rate or CAP rate. The capitalization rate is the rate of return from a real estate investment property based on the income that the property is expected to generate. You use your cap rate to estimate your potential return on the investment. Your cap rate equals your net operating income divided by your current market value. It is not the only factor but important to consider before doing the deal.

Shannon:

Your first real estate investment was in California. Where are you doing most of your investing now?

Perran:

Right now we are doing most of our investing in the Chicago metropolitan area.

Loretta:

In Illinois.

Shannon:

Do you plan on expanding nationwide again?

Loretta:

Here is what I say to that Shannon, we do real estate deals according to the numbers. If the numbers work, we are interested in doing it. Real estate is everywhere, so why limit yourself? The key is are you going to be able to plug into a successful community of real estate investors across the country to make sure you receive the most accurate information. Certainly you can Google Earth the property and take a bird's eye view of what it looks like, but it's nothing like having boots on the ground. It's nothing like determining those little factors, like are there any structures that divide the neighborhood like railroad tracks, special highways or cul-de-sacs? One can do a comparative market analysis (CMA) and have your target property within a half mile radius of sold properties with like attributes but what if you just crossed the street or dividing highway and the properties in that neighborhood aren't going to hold the same after repair value (ARV) than what you are looking at? Those are the little things that you just want to make sure that you are aware of.

Shannon:
Have you ever found a deal that on paper is perfect? All your numbers are there, everything makes sense, but there is just something off that has caused you to walk away?

Loretta:
Yes.

Perran:
I can tell you a story about that...

This is a tax client of mine. He has been doing fix and flipping for about twenty-five years. An individual approached him about a property. Everything that Loretta just talked about—the ARV, the numbers, everything—matched up. The one thing that was not correct with his analysis was that the house was on a busy street. The CMA's were within the surrounding neighborhood, within a block or two, but those houses were on a different street, not a busy street. Consequently, he executed the deal and found out he couldn't sell the property for a profit because of the fact that it was on a busy street. He should have known better. Once you find your niche, do your due diligence both on paper and visiting the property, or it will always end up hurting you in the long run.

Loretta:
The best real estate deals that you can ever do are sometimes the ones that you walk away from.

Shannon:

Do you give that advice to the people you advise?

Loretta:

Yes, and I've had lots of awesome advisors. Although there is one in particular who has always advocated building wealth through long-term real estate and passive income. Thank you Mr. Bob Snyder for your wisdom and guidance! In addition, you can't get emotional about your real estate deals. It's not a pretty pet. This is a business. You've got to do your appropriate analysis and really take a look at the numbers. If the numbers don't work, you walk away. Another deal will come along, it always does.

Perran:

There are always opportunities. My belief is that the economy generates approximately twenty-trillion plus dollars a year. If you can't figure out how to make money in a twenty-trillion-dollar economy, then there is something wrong with your program. There is nothing wrong with the economy. There is never anything wrong with the economy. There is something that needs adjusting with your life plan.

Shannon:

What is the legacy that you want to leave? What will be your legacy?

Loretta:

You want me to go first?

Perran:

Yes, you may.

Loretta:

We want to be able to add value to others so that they can create their lifestyle or whatever they wish to create in their lives. I believe that we were born as creators and, unfortunately in today's society, we have been separated from that creation process due to jobs, stress, etc. I believe we grow up in our society with systems designed to simply plug someone into a cubical at a for-profit corporation rather than tapping into your natural talent to create and contribute to others. The legacy for me has to do with adding value to others. You've got to value people first before you can add value to others. Being remembered after I'm gone for helping and educating others means my legacy lives on.

Part of that legacy is also to create generational wealth, being able to provide your family with resources so that they can choose what they want to create with their life. They can choose a job if it's a job that they like; they can choose being an entrepreneur if that's what they want to do; they can choose creating both paths because they see a void that needs to be filled. If you want to create income, for example, and let's say you love to travel, tell yourself, "I love domestic and international travel! Let me create income that's going to fit the needs of somebody like me and they are willing to pay for this service." I want that flexibility so our family members can choose their lives. We created our business through real estate investing, that's what we love to do while helping others. Certainly, many people helped us out along the way as well.

This is part of paying it forward. The three things that I want people to say about me are: "Loretta is full of love, generosity and practiced her Company's tag line daily—"Everything Is Going To Be OK!"

Perran:

I want to help improve upon people's lives so that they don't stay caught in the rat race. For many people, not being involved in the rat race could be better for everyone. Since we live in America, we should insist upon taking advantage of the many business opportunities placed before us, and a lot of people don't do that. You see, people who aren't from America take advantage of it because they know how it is somewhere else.

In other countries, it is difficult to impossible to start a business. Here, in America, our citizens often fail to see the many opportunities available to them. I want to change that. I want people to see that anyone, regardless of where they were born, or what they were born with, can be successful.

Josh White

Josh White is a late seventies generation X story for the times. Raised and empowered by a single mother, Josh barely squeezed through school and almost didn't Graduate. Josh took the non-academic path to life, found himself uneducated and on his way to hard labor jobs and low pay. Josh worked in the landscaping industry, Professional Motorsports and became a Paramedic/Firefighter. In 2003 Josh's life took a radical twist. He became a father of a beautiful daughter named Madelynn Grace White. This changed everything! In 2004 during a fire training exercise Josh's L5-S1 (lower back) gave out and he was finished! After surgery and rehab he was back at it. This time, Josh was fully engaged with professional motorsports. According to Josh, he had found his place in life. THEN.... 2008 happened. The starting grid went from 43 cars to 12 cars. A little depressing? It was then Josh found himself ready to change his situation for good. Josh ended up working for a few wealthy mentors. He would often ask them, "How did you do this.....?" Many of them had different and multiple companies, start-ups etc. But the one thing Josh found that was a constant with all of them was REAL ESTATE. They ALL invested in REAL ESTATE! The massive and passive income. HE GOT IT!! Understanding this concept, he learned these principles and has been building a portfolio, building businesses, and is completely out of the rat race.

Shannon:
What inspired you to get into real estate?

Josh:
I worked in landscaping/construction and irrigation, installing dream-scapes for some very wealthy people. I was also a firefighter. A lot of the top brass in the department invest in real estate simply because they know that the retirement they're going to receive is not going to be sufficient for the way they want to live. Also, as I was installing water features and elaborate landscapes, no matter what they did as a profession; doctor, lawyer, super sales person, anything they all had one thing in common. They all invested in real estate. That is what opened my eyes about 10 years ago. I knew that I wanted to be in the real estate world.

Shannon:
When you were in their homes did any of them offer up advice?

Josh:
Yes, they told me to get educated!!First, they told me that real estate has been working for thousands of years. Second, they told me if you were to investigate true wealth in this country, not rich; rich and wealth are two different things, every single one of them has their hand in real estate.

Shannon:
Did any of them give you specific advice?

Josh:
Rentals. Start getting rentals, start acquiring rentals at least one or two a year, and never stop working.

That is the new retirement. You need to have investments in real estate because real estate is insured and backed by the real estate. I'm not going to talk bad about the stock market but nothing has insurance. It is a great way to make money if you know what you're doing but nothing is insured. It could crash tomorrow and everybody's money is lost. With real estate the worst case scenario is that you own the property.

Shannon:

They make it sound so easy, "Rentals, acquire one or two a year." That sounds super simple, but how do you do that?

Josh:

There's many different strategies you have to be able to execute to actually have a property become a rental. You can buy it at a deep-down discount and it can need a lot of work, when you're done with it, you have a choice to sell it or keep it and it would become an asset. You need to know a few different strategies to execute, but that all comes down to knowledge and education.

Shannon:

What is the first piece of advice you would give someone who is just starting off in investing?

Josh:

Get educated!! Mostly, would be from a tax and legal point, get yourself structured to do real estate. There's many different entity structures in this country and many different types of Entities and protection. you need to understand the business under the business before you even start out in real estate. That is asset protection, the way credit works and the way the tax is structured. You need to get your own tax structure tailored to you and what you're going to do, not what somebody else tells you to do. The best way to do that is have an interview with a CPA or an attorney and figure out what you're going to do with real estate. That is the first advice I'll give you.

That's the important part. Doing real estate without any of these structures is like getting in a Ferrari with no motor in it and trying drive.

Josh:

You need to start with the first nut and the first bolt and you need to put those two together, and then you go get the next nut and the next bolt. Or if not, you're going to take off and you're going to fall apart.

Shannon:

Is real estate investing success depended on a strong economy?

Josh:

No. Not if your educated. You can make a killing in any market if you have knowledge in your tool belt. There are many different strategies for different times in the market. You can make money in a down-market, you can make money in an up-market, it all takes knowledge and executing responsibility One needs to know the different strategies for the market that is present

Shannon:

What is a good strategy in a down-market if you want to create massive income?

Josh:

A lot of people in the down-market get overstretched during the time and then it crashes. They get overleveraged on their homes and that's when the foreclosures start. A lot of mortgage companies want you to believe that you can afford the home but you really can't. In a down-market, foreclosures and short sales, are the strategy.

The best thing I like about the down-market is you can really, really help people massively and also make massive money. In a foreclosure, you can help them get out of that home or help them save that home. If you help them get out, you can acquire the home. Help them and deal with them to acquire the home, keep a foreclosure out of their life and off of their credit profile. What you've actually done is help them and you've acquired a home for a deep-discount before the bank even got to look at it.

Shannon:

How do you find those people? Is it easy?

Josh:

Relationships!! You can find a list. It's an NOD list or notice of default. You have to create relationships to get them. Good relationships with real estate agents or real estate brokers are essential.

Another thing in a down-market with a foreclosure is rentals. Since a lot of people are getting foreclosed on they need a place to live. You could help them with their home and if you own other real estate, you could help them get back in it!!

Shannon:

It sounds to me like, really, taking care of the people is almost just as important as making money in real estate. Is that accurate?

Josh:

It's more important. The money should only be the receipt for the value created. The money, at least in my business, is result of what I do. A good investor is a problem solver. Every transaction is a problem where it wouldn't be for sale so you find the problem in there and you should solve the problem. That can help to become successful, the money comes after. If you do it for money, some things will work out, some things won't. I tried to model myself after helping first and get the compensation later.

Shannon:

What is the difference between wealthy people and rich people?

Josh:

Rich, is usually fast new money, lottery-type mentalities, individuals that win this, win that. They might find a good product and they'll start a business and sell it and make a loads of money, and go out and buy a lot of depreciating liabilities. That's rich people. It's the education between rich and wealthy. Wealthy people have knowledge and their education is a journey. Rich people... Their education stopped at college. Wealth is something different. Wealth is people thinking of the back side and systems of life versus the front side, in your face. It's a different mindset and it takes a little bit coaching to get that, a lot of personal insight and wanting to learn and personal development to get that away.

The true wealth in this country didn't happen 10 years ago, it happened 60, 70 years ago. The Rockefellers, the Morgans, and Carnegie. That's when wealth started, true wealth. If you find true wealth, if you date it back and you research, it started a long time ago and it's compounding. One thing that makes it clear to me is we say, "Wealth of knowledge" not "Rich of knowledge."

Shannon:
How important do you think it is to have a mentor in real estate?

Josh:
It's vital. It's a team sport. Real estate and investing, it's all a team sport. To do it alone is downright reckless.

Shannon:
Why?

Josh:
Because it's all about relationships. To do it yourself, you're kind of a loner, a shadow. You can do it but it's the relationships that help you gain the good projects and the good deals.

Shannon:
Do you read books on personal development?

Josh:
I read lots of books.

Shannon:
What is your favorite book that you've listened to this year?

Josh:
The Creature from Jekyll Island. Jekyll Island is south of the Georgia coast and all the guys that met there from Charles Schwab, J. P. Morgan, Carnegie and that's how the Federal Reserve was born. A lot of things were very maddening but a lot of things, through getting frustrated, make sense now. Now, I understand the History of currency. It's crazy when you read that book. Every day of your life, you watch things

pass your face that come from that book. It's great knowledge to have to know where the history of money. If you want to be really good in investing in real estate, find the history of money first.

I drive race cars. They say I'm a basket case before I get my car. I get my car and 200 miles an hour and everybody says they feel like I'm asleep because I calm down. I calm down when there's chaos. 200 miles an hour, cars all around me, that's my happy spot, like I wish I could watch my classes in the middle of a race.

I have to listen to my team and my spotter on the radio. I have to know what's going on around me and he does that because I can't turn around to watch.

Shannon:
How are race cars similar to real estate?

Josh:
They go hand in hand. Like I said, if you build your Ferrari without a motor, are you going to go very far? You got to build it from the inside. Ferrari is really ugly if you take the shell off and you can look inside of it, it's like a robot. That's what you have to build before you put your shell on. Then after the shell, you're sexy and you're ready to go.

Shannon:
Are you only doing properties in Utah or investing nationwide?

Josh:
In Washington also. I will invest in deals everywhere; I am not a home body. I'm going to get a couple of flips going here, there is a plethora of opportunity up here.

Shannon:
What is your best strategy for finding fix and flip?

Josh:
Drive for dollars. I like to drive around. I like to find the neighborhoods that I like and I like to drive around. There are other places in

education that you can search for them, you can go to the city county building. Again, that's another relationship that we have to create in real estate is there are lots of brokers out there. You need to get in the network and the relationships is where it starts.

Shannon:

It sounds to me like the brokers and the real estate agents have all of these advantages, why wouldn't you just get your real estate license?

Josh:

Because a real estate license is tax and legal. It's basically to keep us out of jail. A lot of law. Again, if you have the knowledge and you apply it, it is amazing how much you can do on your own?

Shannon:

Do the realtors help you with short sales?

Josh:

Yes.

Shannon:

What is the MLS and why wouldn't you want to buy a house off of something that sounds so official?

Josh:

The MLS is the Multiple Listing Service, it's where homes go to be sold. A lot of times, it's where homes go after everybody looks at them and they're not a deal anymore. They go on the MLS so everybody can see them.

Shannon:

Do most people buy off the MLS or did they know that they should dig?

Josh:

Some people do, some people don't. I know a friend that can find a deal off the MLS in about 15 minutes.

Shannon:

You should have him teach you that.

Josh:

I'm in the process or I can just employ him to do that he's one of my friends and business partners. He's good at it so I let him do that. I'm good at other things.

Shannon:

It's interesting you say that. When you're doing a fix and flip, how much of the work do you do yourself?

Josh:

Absolutely zero.

Shannon:

Is that because you don't know how?

Josh:

No, I do know how but if I was to go and install a window and do it wrong, in order to get that fixed, I have to go talk to myself in the mirror and tell myself to fix it. If I have a professional do it, it's also guaranteed. If I do it, it's not guaranteed, it's not insured. I go and get a license and bonded insured professionals to do the work.

You spend more money doing the work yourself because you're spending not only the money but you're spending your time and that's the most ... If I were doing what we're doing, we're using money as the tool and time is the reason. Right?

Shannon:

Yeah. Do you think it ever benefits to do the work yourself?

Josh:

There's things you can do, if you have an afternoon, I'm not the boss, the contractor is the boss. I like to learn how to do that stuff, stuff like that, paint. The stuff that needs tools and the stuff that needs craftsmanship,

Shannon:

Nice. Short sales, are you comfortable talking about short sales?

Josh:

Been involved in a couple. It's not a short sale, it should be called the long purchase, I know that.

Shannon:

Okay. Why? How long will it take? I thought they were supposed to be short.

Josh:

No. The word short is shorting the bank on the price, that's the only meaning for short

You're trying to talk to the bank to come up on a price and it's usually short of the actual price. They're trying to get it off their books. See, banks don't want these homes in their portfolio because they have to pay taxes on them so they will short sale it to you. Most of the time it is a win, win.

Shannon:

Is there a common percentage or a dollar amount that you should go offer the bank when you are going in to try and get a short sale?

Josh:

It's all situational, location and type of property.

Shannon:

Why?

Josh:

Because we're going to try to get the short in the bank but now since, I don't know, 2010, 2011, we have depreciation, correct?

The banks can't short them this much now because it's Appreciated. Not that much room to short.

Shannon:

Do you find the short sales on that MLS list?

Josh:

Yes, you can. I have an agent up here in Seattle that has her own brokerage but she works for the bank so she has this whole file cabinet full of these short sales that aren't even on the MLS. They're in a file cabinet.

Shannon:

Well, that should be interesting especially doing it in Seattle. How much time do you think you'll need to spend up there?

Josh:

Well, I have my sister that is a brand new real estate investor. She is going to take care of a lot of the marketing up here and find projects up here. I'm just going to be going back and forth from Utah. I'm not doing any rehabs in Utah right now, I'm looking to do them up here because I'm building a team in Seattle. And teaching my sister the game.

Shannon:

I love that you called it a game, why do you call it that?

Josh:

Because it's fun and you constantly have to practice and play your best hand You constantly have to perform, you can't get complacent. You can sit on the sidelines or you can jump in, it's a choice.

Shannon:

Love it. Your goal is to always win the game?

Josh:

Well, not always win the game but always play well, how about that? Sometimes it not whether you win or lose. But how you played…

Shannon:

I like that. That's a concept we're teaching our kids right now. It's not about winning and losing, it's how you play the game.

Josh:

Yeah, sports. There's a few times ... Football and hockey, I played the best game in my life but we lost.

Shannon:

Yup, that is very true. What type of legacy do you want to leave?

Josh:

I want to leave a legacy of honesty and responsibility. I would like to leave a legacy that has taught people how to create wealth and create systems to achieve Faith, family, fitness and finances. How to create wealth, and how not to depend on outside influences, family, state, or government. One of my biggest goals is that I want to create entrepreneurial schools for children. Teach them to take the knowledge and apply their talents to create true wealth. I want to create spaces for Entrepreneurial children to gain knowledge and education. I also want a BIG wake. That means I had some kind of meaning.

Shannon:

Patience is a virtue, right?

Josh:

Yes, especially in real estate. Well, sometimes you got to have a ready, fire, aim mentality. You fire and then aim. If you sit and over analyze a deal to try to figure out the numbers... when you go back, it's going to be gone. That's how you have to approach deals sometimes. Go Get It!!

Shannon:

Are you going to do any of the multi-family dwellings?

Josh:

Yes, I intend to own many. Also, the demographic that's happening, the baby boomers. 80% of them have less than $2,000 in the savings account, which is very alarming, so what they're doing is moving in with their children.

Shannon:

Yeah, I didn't think about that.

Josh:

Hospice is more expensive than owning a home. It's more economical to bring them home and take care of them.

Hugh & Jessica Zaretsky

Hugh Zaretsky is a Real Estate Investment expert, technology specialist and distinguished Author. He is also a trained professional speaker who has trained over 10,000 real estate investors and spoken for many national organizations. Hugh's engaging presentations encompass a wide variety of real estate investment, technology, leadership, sales and marketing topics.

Jessica Zaretsky is first and foremost a teacher with a degree a bachelor of education. Her passion is helping people see the options they have in their life. She has been recognized as a national sales and marketing trainer for several different organizations. For the last eight years she has been a real estate investor and mentor. Together Hugh and Jessica have built teams of real estate investors from New York to Hawaii

Contact Info:
Email: Hugh@hughzaretsky.com
jessicazaretsky@outlook.com
Web: www.hughandjessciazaretsky.com
www.studyforeclosures.com
www.happyhealthwealthyfamily.com
www.hughzaretsky.com
best.statueofresponsibility.org

Shannon:

What inspired you two to get into real estate?

Hugh:

For me, it was 9/11 and I was here, in New York City. I worked less than five blocks away from the World Trade Center, and I had just moved in to New York City on September 1st, 2001. I worked for a company called Getty Images at that time; I was the Director of Technology. My job was to get every picture that came in to Getty Images out to every major newspaper in under five minutes. On 9/11, both planes flew over our building, and we looked right out into the Twin Towers. Nobody had digital cameras on their cell phones back then, and the company wanted photos of the scene, so I grabbed the ID name badge camera we had in the IT department. I brought it over to the picture desk and they said, "Take it to the roof, give it to the photographer." I took it to the roof with one of the editors but there was no photographer there. The editor didn't want to take the picture. So, I ended up taking the first pictures of the scene that went out to every major newspaper.

I watched people go to work with hopes and dreams that day, and they never got a chance to fulfill them. Right then I said, "You know, I've got to change what I'm doing. I've got to stop putting off my dreams until tomorrow." I won't tell the whole 9/11 story; it was a really rough day. You know, it just made me rethink everything. Everything. So after 9/11, I started looking for an opportunity. I found real estate investing in 2003, and I've been having a great time teaching and training over 10,000 real estate investors across the country and helping them "Fire Their Boss!"

Shannon:

What got you into real estate investing?

Jessica:

I was working two, sometimes three, jobs at a time, and I was the primary breadwinner of my household. I was also going to school full time. At one time I was working at Mercedes Benz, and I would watch these people walk in and plop down $80,000 cash for cars. I saw all these people who were business owners and real estate investors and I'm sitting there making my $50,000 a year wage and thinking, "There's got to be a better way. I'm working two or three jobs to stay afloat, to provide some kind of a lifestyle for my kids here, but there's got to be a better way."

I was very into watching HGTV back then. These guys were making $20,000 profits, $50,000 profits, and it looked so easy! I went and found a friend of a friend through somebody at work that was a real estate agent and started going out with her to properties. In 2006, when you could just sign your name and get a mortgage, you didn't have to have any money down, and within a span of three to four months, I purchased two properties. I intended to live in one and rent out the other rooms. I was single at the time and it made sense. Life changed and I ended up getting engaged and married to my now ex-husband. We couldn't afford to live in that property that I had already bought without renting out the rooms. Together, we looked for a different property that we could buy, live in part of it, fix it up, and then rent out the other part of it as a two-family home while we fixed it up in order to flip it. Both of those ended up being not good deals... until I got educated and was able to turn them around.

Shannon:
Hugh, did you also do any bad deals before you started getting educated, or did you just start with education first?

Hugh:
I started with education first. In 2003 I learned one little real estate investment strategy, and I was able to acquire my condo in New York City $50,000 under market. In 2003 the market had fully recovered from 9/11. It was actually screaming, and people said," You can't buy property under value." I bought my condo $50,000 under value, and by the time we closed on it, I was up another $50,000 in equity. So, I made about half my salary at my job, and I didn't have to work sixty to eighty hour weeks. I'm from New York and I'm a bit skeptical, so I decided to learn a little more about real estate investing. It took me until 2005 to fire my boss and walk away from my job.

Shannon:

How has real estate education changed the way you invest?

Jessica:

Once I got involved with real estate investment education and started learning, we actually turned both of those deals around to be good deals. The point of buying the two-family was so that we could move into it, rent it out while we fixed it up, and then we were going to sell it as a fix and flip and make a profit. Well, halfway through the project, after sinking $20,000 into it, we realized that it needed $40,000 worth of work! I was scrambling to try to find more money to put into this property, and then the market crashed. All of a sudden it was worth $70,000 less than what I'd paid for it.

I put renters in the house, but even after that we were still paying $500 to $800 a month out of pocket every single month in order to keep it from going to foreclosure. I kept that up for six years; I had just resigned myself. I said, "Well, you know, in thirty years, when it's paid off, then I'll finally make some money on this thing." Then, one day my friend called me up and told me about a group of real estate investors that could potentially help me out with my property. When I came down to meet them, I met people who would mentor me. I started going through investing classes, and we actually turned the deal around. We negotiated with the bank; I didn't even know you could do that until I got educated. We turned the mortgage around so that I actually could live in part of it and rent the other part of it, and the rent covered the entire mortgage, so I got to live in my house for eighteen months for free.

Once I moved to New York, the market had started to come back and we decided to sell my house. Because of the way my mentors had helped me negotiate the deal, I was able to sell it and make a profit of $38,754. Education turned this deal completely around.

Shannon:

Do you find that most real estate investors are also real estate agents? Do you feel like it is better to be a real estate agent and an investor?

Hugh:

In my opinion, if you're already a real estate agent when you start down the path to becoming an investor, awesome. Keep your license. There are some benefits to it, but there are also some liabilities that come with it. Legally, when an agent makes offers there are a few more rules. Plus, you also have to deal with your own individual broker. If you're not an agent or broker, you don't have to worry about the extra rules. As an agent, you get access to the MLS to find properties but you have more liability that comes with it because you have to disclose that you're an agent when you're buying any property.

I've passed my New York state real estate agent exam and the school exam so I could file my license in 2008 or 2009 to become an agent, but I chose not to because I didn't want that added liability. If I make an offer or Jess makes an offer, we're just average Joes. Once you have a license, the state puts you at that higher level and says you're an "expert." If you take advantage of somebody, or if somebody feels like you took advantage of them, they could go after your license, your business, and your profit because you are an expert in the eyes of the state. In my opinion it is not worth the hassle.

Jessica:

I think it's so individual at this point. We've got a guy who's been within our real estate investing community for a long time who just chose to go get his license. We, Hugh and I, were thinking, "Wow, he's going to take this liability on? He's going to have to check in with a broker. He's already doing all these deals, now he's going to have to check in every time he does a deal." He, on the other hand, felt like there was all this money he could make as an agent on top of his investing, which would offset the liability. To each his own. Hugh and I don't want that stress.

Shannon:
Do you guys have a favorite exit strategy and why?

Hugh:

For over ten years of teaching and training real estate investors, I have taught all my people how to have different exit strategies. None of us are psychics. We don't know if the market's going to change, what's going to happen. Currently we've got the election going on. After the election there are all sorts of rumors about what is going to happen. You've got to make sure that you are set up with multiple exit strategies. Having three exit strategies always allows you that option to have a backup plan and have a backup plan for the backup plan. If you're doing a fix and flip and the market crashes, you're still going to make money renting it out, if you've done your deal correctly. If renting isn't your favorite option, you've got other strategies you can use.

After the crash from 2008 to 2010, it changed the way everybody evaluated properties. Unfortunately, right now we have some people going back to those old ways, saying, "Hey, the market is going to keep going up and I'm going to flip property and make a killing!" One of the biggest things is to make sure the property cash flows, one way or another, whether I can do it on a lease option, I can do it on owner financing, or just a straight rental.

One of those has to be your exit strategy, especially in today's world, because when the market crashes, if I'm cash flowing $500 a month and my property drops half in value, I don't really care because I know every single month between the first and the fifth I'm getting paid $500. Whether that's for the lease option, whether that's for the owner financing, whatever happens to me, I know I can cash flow it, so I've got that back up. I can afford to hold that property until the market starts to come back to where I need it to be to sell it. There's got to be one of those strategies in there for investors to make sure they 'CYA': cover your assets.

Shannon:

What is your view on whether you should invest locally or it's okay to invest in other areas?

Jessica:

I'm very comfortable investing outside of my own area as long as I've done my research. Because we have a community of real estate investors nationwide, it makes it easier to invest outside of our local areas because we've got feet on the ground that can say, "Oh yeah, this is the experience I've had in this area," or, "This is the experience I've had with this property manager. Look at this guy. This is a great inspector." It makes it easier because of our network to invest outside of our area. I'm perfectly comfortable with it, and then Hugh has ownership in properties across the country. I would say we're pretty comfortable with that.

Hugh:
I have always invested in different markets. You need to invest in the different markets to meet your investment goals. In New York City here, it'll probably blow you away, but we pay $1200 or $1300 per square foot. When you're talking about a 675 square-foot apartment, that's worth just shy of a million dollars. You're not going to cash flow that unless you put down a lot of cash, so if you're looking for a rental property, if you're looking for cash flow, you have to go outside the area.

New York City is one of those places that you invest in for appreciation and to protect your money from market downturns. Of course, you could invest in New York City and if the US market crashes, then Europeans, the Japanese, or the Chinese come in and buy the properties, so the values aren't going down. You're going to play the New York City market for appreciation. Depending on what your goal is, you need to adjust where you invest across the country.

Jessica:
We teach our students, specifically here in New York, how to invest well outside of the area because of that fact.

Hugh:
Yeah, the average student coming in isn't able to afford a million-dollar condo right out of the gate. They're going to need to go to another market across the country, invest, build up that cash flow, build up savings, and then come back and park money here. We have 186 units across the country. We're looking at investments in Southern Illinois, Florida, North Carolina and a few other places. For us it's more about if it's a good deal versus where it is. Jessica and I have built our business so it is automated, where we have people calling us. We get phone calls all the time saying, "Hey, look. We got a guy, he's got ten properties and

he's in trouble. Can you guys help him?" We will then go in put a deal together that is a win-win. If it is a large bulk OREO acquisition, then we often allow our team and members to invest in the deal with us. We have completed a 33-property, a 59-unit, and a 65-unit acquisition as well as raised over $1,800,000 in a PPM and turned that into $4,500,000 worth of real estate.

With a PPM, we are required by law to file with the Security and Exchange Commission (SEC). It was like creating our own little mini-hedge fund.

The nice thing is that there's less than $500,000 worth of debt on that PPM portfolio. For us, for me, it's about the deal. If it's a good deal, we'll run the numbers, or as Jessica said, if it's near our community or team members then we already have people there. We don't have to learn the area. I could just pick up the phone and say, "Hey, we got a deal here, what do you think about it?"

Jessica:
Then we just double check everything.

Hugh:
The next time you want to buy a car, here's what you're going to do. You're going to call us up and we'll tell you to go buy a house in the Midwest for $40,000. Take that money you would pay cash for a car and use it to generate a cash flow of $450 a month. You're going to take that $450 cash flow and you're going to use that to lease a car, and now your house is paying for your car. Then, every three years you can turn it in and get a new car, and write it off on your business as a tax deduction.

Jessica:
I love it when people get the fire. They get the fire and they get so excited about real estate, and Hugh and I love that because we love the passion. Then we can just say, "Now hold up. Take a breath, and let me tell you what not to do so you don't have to go through what we did." Both Hugh and I have made mistakes and gone through challenges and dealt with things. We want to make sure that people

don't repeat the same mistakes that we've made. Passion can create some mistakes. It can create the emotional buying.

Hugh:
That is the number one mistake that most investors make. They buy on emotion versus numbers.

Jessica:
Emotional buying is number one, and I think a close second is pride, thinking you know more than you do, not being open to more education, learning new things. I watch even seasoned investors make stupid mistakes because they just think they know it all.

Hugh:
The biggest thing when people run their numbers is that the numbers never lie but sometimes people stretch the truth. When somebody's emotional about something, they'll run the numbers on their property and then go back and change it because there's not enough profit. They'll go massage their numbers: maybe I won't spend that much, maybe I won't have to do that much work. That always comes back to bite them; I always tell people, if you really love a property and you have to have it, then buy it, and move into your new house.

Otherwise you buy it based on numbers. I don't care if it's got a purple bathroom, shag carpet, whatever. It's based on numbers only. That's how you can help people separate their emotions from the deal. On their second deal they are less emotional and it is easier to help them separate their emotions.

Shannon:
If you had only one piece of advice that you could give someone, what would it be?

Jessica:
Never stop learning. Never get to that place where you feel like you know it all. If you think you've got it down, you don't have anything left to learn, that's the moment you're about to walk into a bad deal.

Shannon:
Hugh, how about you?

Hugh:
A piece of advice I would give to everybody is this: real estate investing really has no rules. It can be as creative as you want it to be. People are used to just one little straight way of doing something, but there's thousands of different ways when you do it. You can be as creative as you want on a deal to set it up so that it's a win-win for everybody. Too many people try to take advantage of people, but that's not the way to do it. If you get real creative with your real estate, it might take a little while to get there, but you'll have the most success and you're going to see better results. Long-term people that you can call on a moment's notice, a past tenant, somebody else like that, they'll call you back up with a referral. Get creative!

Shannon:
When you guys think about what you are building now and why you're doing it, sum up for me your "why." What is the legacy that you want to leave behind?

Jessica:
I've watched money handed to children just ruin their future, ruin their ability to learn to work. Nobody handed me money. I was always searching for the answer. What's the answer? What's the secret? What's the secret to being wealthy? What's the secret to making money? I'd been searching, searching, and searching and learning, learning, learning. My goal is to first of all be able to teach my children how the process works of making money, not just here's a lump sum but how to actually do it. I've always loved being a teacher. My degree is in teaching; I have a passion for teaching. If I could show the world how to actually learn the secrets of money and create wealth, and put it into a step by step system, that would be unbelievable to me because there's so many people out there looking for the answers, and it's just a matter of showing people a realistic way to get there.

Hugh:

My life has gone through some changes over the past couple years. One of those changes was getting ready for Jessica and the boys to move to New York City. It's funny, I come from three generations of teachers. My grandfather was a teacher; both my parents were teachers; my sister's a teacher; I married a teacher. It's always been about what we give back. Growing up with parents that were teachers, we had a lot of time freedom, but not financial freedom. I've watched different generations grow up and most people don't understand how to use money. That's why we love the Statue of Responsibility Movement, because it's talking about sharing with adults and kids how to think differently about money. It's funny, eight-year-old Caston comes to our Cashflow game nights, and he beats the adults because he's thinking like an investor. Most adults haven't learned to think like an investor; they think like employees.

If we can change our mindset and the mindset of our children, then we can leave that legacy for future generations; that is really what it's about. How can we change the world and make it a better place? Hence, Jessica and I have aligned ourselves with the Statue of Responsibility that will teach children responsibility and financial knowledge from a very young age, as well as get out there and talk to more adults about financial responsibility. It is never too late to learn. It's sad that for the majority of our country, you go to school and learn how to dissect a pig or a frog, but you don't learn how to balance your finances or even your checkbook. You don't learn how to use interest rates. You don't learn any of those things in our school system. It's nothing against teachers, it's just how the system is set up. Many know the Pythagorean theorem, but they don't know if they've got enough money in their checking account. They don't know how to save for something that they want. We need to help future generations get a better start in life. That will be my legacy: teaching tens of thousands of people how to invest in real estate and use money the right way.

Woody Woodward

Woody Woodward dropped out of high school at age 16, was a millionaire by 26 and flat broke by age 27. After clawing his way out of financial ruin he built four different multi-million dollar companies before he turned 40. Through overcoming this adversity Mr. Woodward has become a best-selling author of fifteen books about turning tragedy into triumph. Having interviewed over 2,500 people around the world for his research, he is the pioneer and founder of *Your Emotional Fingerprint*™. Understanding this cutting edge human technology allows one to strip back the layers of excuses and build a proper foundation for mass achievement in one's personal life, relationships and career. Emotional Fingerprint was chosen as one of the leading techniques to be presented to the United Nations to assist them in reaching their millennial goals.

His latest project is inspiring entrepreneurs with M.O.N.E.Y. Matrix™ daily videos that help them reach their goals, make more money and find fulfillment in their careers. He has shared his cutting edge techniques on ABC, CBS, NBC, FOX and Forbes.

Contact Info:
www.GetMoneyMatrix.com
www.MeetWoody.com

Shannon:

According to Forbes Magazine, real estate is one of the top three ways that people become wealthy. As a real estate expert, why do you feel that this is the case?

Woody:

Real estate is the only investment I know of where you have a tangible, physical product that, even if the market goes down, you can still use. Yes, you can say stocks are tangible, but in reality they're not. Yes, you can lease them out, you can do calls and you can do puts on them, but with real estate, even if the market crashes, you can physically rent that property. You get a tax write-off if you are renting the property; so to me, real estate has always been, looking back in history, one of the top ways to generate revenue.

Shannon:

Do you have an opinion on whether commercial real estate or residential real estate is a better investment?

Woody:

I have friends who do both. I personally have always done residential. As for my friends who do commercial real estate it adds a zero to their net worth. If you're going to make a hundred thousand dollars on flipping a residential property, you'll make about a million flipping a commercial property; so it's the same game, just bigger numbers. If you have the resources to do it, most billionaires do it in commercial property, not residential. A lot of millionaires do residential property.

Shannon:

How hard is it to get started in residential real estate if you don't have a lot of money?

Woody:

That's the great thing about residential versus commercial; it doesn't take hardly anything with residential. Nowadays, you can still put down 3 percent or 5 percent on a home to buy it and then flip it, or to let it appreciate and sell it in the future and make additional revenue by leasing it, or there are a lot of different techniques where you can do owner financing. Owner financing is when the seller can't sell a home, maybe it's a bad market, and they're willing to carry that note for you; so in essence, the seller becomes the bank and you're buying it directly from the seller. You then still have all the legal rights to that property, so you can rent it out, you can fix it up, you can sell it; you can do whatever you want, as long as the seller's paid in full when you sell that home.

Shannon:
When the seller's paid in full, how does that benefit them if they're the bank? How do they buy another house?

Woody:
There is only one of two reasons why a seller will finance, in my experience. First is that they have enough income on their own, but they're happy just to sell it because they want to get a higher interest rate. Right now, if you put your money in the bank, you're going to get maybe 1 or 1.5 percent. If they carry the note on that home for you, they can charge you 5, 7, even 10 percent, so they're making more money on their own money, so they become a bank.

The other reason is that sometimes in a bad market they just can't sell a home. Let's say they owe $200,000 on a home and the home's only worth $175,000, so they physically can't sell it unless they come up with the $25,000 difference; so they'll carry their loan for you, and then as the market changes and goes back up and the home's worth $250,000, you can then sell it and keep that extra $50,000 since you bought it for $200,000. Then they are happy because now they get their $200,000 out that they already owe their bank, and it becomes a little win-win.

Shannon:
When you're actually looking for homes in a down market situation where people are upside down in their homes, do you look at the location? Do you look at the future projections for businesses, neighborhoods, etc.?

Woody:

Absolutely. The number one thing that you hear people always talk about with real estate, the number one technique, is location, location, location. I've had friends who have literally bought corner lots and then they heard that Walmart was coming across the street. This happened to a friend of mind in California who bought the lot for $150,000 and had the owner carry the note. Six months later Walmart announced that they were building across the street. His lot went from $150,000 to $500,000 literally overnight. He would be able to sell that and take that money. Now he can play in the commercial business on a little bit larger level.

Most investor works the same way. You make a little bit, you turn that money over. It's really called compounding interest where you take your principle and your interest and then you roll it over again into the next property. There's also a great tax benefit to that as well. You don't have to pay tax on that money as long as you're rolling it over in to a property of equal or higher value.

Shannon:
What do you think is the number one mistake that an individual makes when buying their first investment property?

Woody:

The number one reason why people make mistakes on their first investment property is they don't have a mentor. They don't have someone to follow. They don't have someone that can show them the right thing to do. They just hear their buddies doing it, they go out and they buy a home, but they haven't done all the certification, they haven't verified that this property's not going to have termite issues or meth issues, or something else that could really hurt them. They think, "Oh, it's a good deal, I can buy that and make a ton of money." The benefit to real estate is there's tons of people and there's tons of organizations out there that have already done it a thousand times, so connect with them. Join an investment club, join a company that does education, and then they'll help you limit your potential risk.

Shannon:

How have your mentors in real estate investing helped you to navigate pitfalls?

Woody:

We don't know what we don't know, and every deal has a potential problem, and every deal tends to really have a problem. I'm in the middle of a transaction right now where the home had to be lifted. We knew that there were some cracks in the foundation, but we weren't sure; so before we actually took ownership and before we actually even wrote the contract, we had an engineer come out. The only reason I did that is my mentor recommended, "You know what Woody, if you've got cracks in your foundation that are larger than average, hire an engineer. Spend the six, seven, eight hundred dollars. You'll save hundreds of thousands of dollars of potential losses for a small investment", so we did that and it ended up costing the seller $75,000 to raise that foundation. Had we bought that home not knowing that, we'd be out $75,000, so an $800 investment saved me $75,000.

Now, after the home was raised, we paid another $400 for an inspector to go out and verify absolutely everything. What he did is he pulled off all of the insulation in the basement and found another crack that we didn't know about, so now we're having another company come out and verify that crack because you can see daylight through the foundation. That's never good. You never want to see daylight in the foundation.

They're coming out to fix that. Once again, the seller will have to pay that and we won't.

Shannon:

How do you help other people learn more about real estate?

Woody:

Everybody has that friend who is in real estate. I'm that friend for my friends, and they will always ask me, "Woody what about this?" Or, "What about that transaction? What about that home you flipped?" What I like to do is just invite them to come along and take a look.

There's times where I'll take five of my friends and show them a house that I'm doing, show them the pitfalls and mistakes, and where's the benefit to changing it.

This one home, there is about $100,000 in equity from us just buying it right. I believe that when it comes to real estate, you make your money when you buy it, not when you sell it, so you have to buy it right.

Shannon:
You are obviously passionate about real estate. What actually inspired you to get into the industry?

Woody:
I grew up with my folks in a different generation where my dad was the traditional father who would always work and my mother would stay home. In the 80's when the market crashed and we didn't have a lot of money, it was a challenge, and so my mom became a realtor. She would list homes, so when I was very young, I'd go with my mom when she would go list a home. I'd walk through these homes and they were, to a kid, like a jungle gym. They were just so fascinating, and I grew up being exposed to real estate. I met some of the investors who my mom was selling for and it changed my life forever.

If you list a home as a typical realtor, you'll make 3 percent. The investor can make 10 to 20 percent. They're just taking the greater risk. The realtor doesn't have any risk. They have some advertising costs, but that's not a huge risk. The investor who bought the home, fixed it up, put new paint/carpet in, now is making $50,000, $100,000, $150,000 on a transaction. That blew my mind, and that was the second I knew I wanted to be in real estate.

Shannon:
What are some of the creative ways that you use now, or what is your favorite way to find a property to acquire a fix and flip?

Woody:
For me the best way to find property is to know your area, so back to location, location, location. The home that I'm buying right now, the

one that had the sunken basement, we've been trying for two years to get this home. We've talked to the seller, he wouldn't sell it to us. Then low and behold we found out that he passed away, and then we went to his heirs, which was his older sister. Well, she's eighty-four years old. She doesn't want to deal with this property. She lives out of state, but because I was driving around, just driving by this one house that I've always wanted to acquire, I saw a car there. I knew he lived out of state. It was an investment property for him, so when I saw a car there, I just knocked on the door. And told them that because the home had been vacant for over three years, that's why it was neglected and the home sunk. Basically, I was able to get the home before it even went on the market.

Had they taken the time to invest in the property, to fix it up, and then to sell it, I would've been out of the loop. So to me the best technique is, take an area, a geographical area that you know well and trust, and then master it. Know every house. You can pull titles. You can find out when people are delinquent. You can ask them to buy the home before it goes into foreclosure. There are so many techniques to save yourself time because it's trying to find that jewel in the rough. It's always hard to find, but when you find one, you can pull out fifty to a hundred grand.

Shannon:
How do you decide if you are going to fix and flip a home or buy and hold it for rental income?

Woody:
If I'm in a financial position where I can hold it and I can keep it long-term and I believe a certain area geographically is going to go up in value, then I will hold it. I have done holds in the past, but on the fix and flips, those are the ones that give you large pops. Wealthy people, I believe, get wealthy by the large pops–fifty grand, a hundred grand, two hundred and fifty grand pops. I've made $200,000 on a house in thirty days. I can't save that much money myself, I can't save my way to wealth, and I don't believe most people can. You look at CEOs who have large stock options and a buyout takes place; they

get a large pop of millions of dollars, so to create massive wealth, you've got to have large pops.

Well, as soon as you've had enough large pops where you've got a good nest egg, now you can afford to buy one, hold it, and if a renter does not pay, you can afford to make that monthly payment. I don't believe in being house poor. If you own a bunch of properties but you can't fix up the yard or you can't take a vacation, I call that being house poor. You may have a million dollars in real estate, but you can't afford to take a vacation, then you don't have the life that real estate's designed to give you.

Shannon:

I'd like to go back to when you said you saw the car and you just knocked on the door. Tell me how that conversation went?

Woody:

It's very simple. You can tell when somebody is stressed. You can see it on their face. This woman looked bewildered. This is the first time she had seen this home after her brother passed. She didn't want that property. She lives two thousand miles away. She wants nothing to do with this property. I asked her, "You know what, I've been watching this home for two years. Are you the new owner? She said, "Yeah, my brother passed, and now I have inherited this home." I said, "Well, what is your intention? Do you want to sell the home, or do you want to keep it and rent it out? What would you like to do?" "Oh my gosh, I just want to sell this home," she replied, so I gave her an offer on the spot. She turned it down. I waited about a month. I kept checking on the home. I saw them doing yard work trying to fix it up. I went back to her, I said, "You know what, are you by chance interested in selling the home yet?" At that point, she was, because she just realized how much work it was going to be to fix it up.

You have to understand that if someone is going to sell you a house at a discount than what it should be going for, that means there's inherently something wrong with the home. Either it needs new carpet, or they had pets in there, or it smells. It's been neglected. Things are broken. So when you're looking for a fix and flip, they're never in perfect condition, otherwise they'd get top of the retail value. People who have these homes don't want them because they know how much it's going to cost to fix it, and that was the case with her, so it was really easy to buy it from her, to take that pressure and stress off of her.

Shannon:

Do you think that you can have real estate success being a one- man-show, or do you think that most people need to have a team?

Woody:

When I say I'm a one-man show I don't want to imply that I don't have a team and I don't work with other people because that's not true. I don't have employees that I pay that help me run my company, but I have a network of people that I work with. In real estate you cannot be successful without a network of people. It's impossible. You need to know a title guy, a realtor. You need to know an appraiser. There are so many moving parts in real estate, you need to have a group of people you work with.

When it comes to education, I go back to that saying, "We don't know what we don't know." Create an environment and a network, facilitate a mastermind, put people who are in real estate in the same room and you will expedite your knowledge. You'll expedite your learning curves. It is crucial that you spend time with a team of people who have your best interest in mind to make you successful.

Shannon:

What is your favorite investment strategy when the market is good and homes are selling quickly?

Woody:

In California in 2005 when the market was just exploding and homes were appreciating at 30 percent a year, if you bought a home for $400,000, in a year it was going for a $520,000, so in that market we were buying homes that weren't even built yet. When a new subdivision was under construction we would put down $5,000. Homes would take six months to nine months to build. By the time we bought that home and moved into it, we already had $60,000 to $80,000 of appreciation; so in an up market my favorite thing to do is speculation. Know an area, know where the parks and schools are being built, buy homes that are under construction so that you can flip them as soon as you close on them.

Shannon:
When you look at everything that you do in your life, your real estate investing career, your entrepreneurial adventures, and your life married with children, what legacy do you want to leave?

Woody:
I want my children and the people that I have the opportunity to come in contact with to realize that they can change. Regardless of your past, regardless of where you started, you can change. I believe real estate is one of the greatest agents for change. It allows someone, even an uneducated person like myself, to learn something, to master something, and then to make a very good income with it.

My legacy is that I want people to realize they can do it. That's the bottom line, that they can have their own life, that they can change, that they can become who they want to become regardless of their background.

As my wife would say, "We are just borrowing it for a time before the next generation borrows it." Since we don't take anything with us, I would want my legacy to be the impact I have had on my relationships. There is no doubt my life has been better because of the lives of others. I would like to do the same for someone else.

CPSIA information can be obtained
at www.ICGtesting.com
Printed in the USA
FFOW02n0137301217
44188552-43608FF

9 780998 234014